MASTERING
PERSONAL
GROWTH

MASTERING
PERSONAL
GROWTH

Maxie Dunnam
Gordon MacDonald
Donald W. McCullough

Christianity Today, Inc.

MASTERING PERSONAL GROWTH
© 1992 by Christianity Today, Inc.
Published by Multnomah Press
Sisters, Oregon 97759

Printed in the United States of America.

Library of Congress Cataloging-in-Publication Data

Dunnam, Maxie E.
      Mastering personal growth / Maxie D. Dunnam, Gordon
MacDonald, Donald W. McCullough.
         p. cm. — (Mastering ministry)
      ISBN 0-88070-526-4
    I. MacDonald, Gordon. II. McCullough, Donald W., 1949-
III. Title. IV. Series.
BV4011.6.D86 1992
248.8'92—dc20   92-20475
                                                    CIP

92 93 94 95 96 97 98 99 00 01 - 10 9 8 7 6 5 4 3 2 1

Contents

Introduction

My wife recently bought me a plant for my office. She, the horticulturist of the family, was trying to nurture the nurturing qualities of her left-brained husband. This was an act of faith on her part. The last time she gave me a plant, it was silk.

"That way you won't have to remember to water it," she had said dryly.

Very funny, I thought. No doubt she was remembering the previous twenty-three plants she'd presented me, only three of which survived the first month (although not the second).

She also recognized my impulsive nurturing style. Others call it the benign-neglect-then-panic school of gardening. The first few days go well as I tend my plant meticulously. But busyness sets in, and I ignore it. I notice, however, that nothing untoward happens to the plant — not the reinforcement a gardener of my ilk needs.

Soon the plant is without water a week or two, until I notice the leaves yellowing and drooping. Immediately I dump a bucket of water on my "baby," all five inches of it. After it recovers from shock, it returns to lush green health again. I breathe a sigh of relief and begin another period of benign neglect, before panic sets in once more.

Funny thing: that's often how I nurtured myself as a pastor. In seminary, upon hearing stories about yellowing and wilting pastors, I vowed to attend to my own personal growth. After all, if I wasn't growing, how could I expect to last in ministry? And how could I expect my congregation to grow?

But the busyness of ministry gradually shoved Bible and theology reading off my daily to-do list. Not soon afterwards, my prayer life began to suffer.

Frankly, I was surprised at how well I could get by skipping personal disciplines a day or two . . . or three . . . or four.

Within a couple of weeks, I began withering, whereupon I desperately hungered and thirsted for righteousness. So, like a famished man, I gorged myself on a feast of devotional reading and prayer, reordered my goals and priorities, made great plans for a new, balanced ministry — whereupon a combination of my own sloth and the demands of ministry would kick in another cycle.

In talking with colleagues, I discovered I wasn't alone. That's only part of the struggle pastors face when it comes to personal growth. How do you find time for personal growth, especially the more demanding disciplines of concentrated prayer and theological reading? If you can get away, what should you do with your time? Is physical fitness all that important to ministry, and if so, what form can it take for a harried pastor?

To address — constructively — such concerns, we've brought together three men in this volume of Mastering Ministry who know well the challenges of both effective ministry and personal growth.

Maxie Dunnam

If we didn't know better, we would have thought Maxie Dunnam was a southern gentleman.

He came out to the reception area to meet us LEADERSHIP editors warmly when we came to his office to talk about this book. As we walked the hallway, he stopped to greet three or four people, riveting his eyes and warm smile on each. His spacious office was punctuated with fine art — some Marc Chagall reprints hung above the couch he sat upon. He began our conversation by modestly wondering, in a lazy drawl, what he would have to offer this book.

Then he took his shoes off. And he put his feet on the glass coffee table — this was no typical southern gentlemen addicted to the formalities of southern culture.

Then he began talking about his own struggles and successes with his own personal growth — he was no landed gentry who took life as it came.

Instead, he is a man of Wesleyan intensity and joy.

We learned this had been born in him some years earlier when he had been struggling. He had been invited to attend one of E. Stanley Jones's famous Christian ashrams — retreat centers for study and meditation.

"I remember vividly the experience at an altar at the close of the ashram," he recalled. "Brother Stanley asked probingly, 'Do you want to be whole?' He said the only possibility for wholeness was the indwelling Christ. I responded longingly and with certainty, 'Yes!'

"I yielded myself more completely than ever to Christ, inviting him to live his life in me. And I made a new commitment to ministry, a ministry in which I would allow Christ to live *through* me, rather than me ministering *for* Christ."

Thus the connection between the outward and inner Maxie Dunnam: he's gracious *and* intense because he knows himself as not just the servant of Christ but also the dwelling place of Christ.

This joyous intensity has undergirded all of Maxie's subsequent ministry. He has been an editor with *The Upper Room* and has served churches in California, Georgia, and Mississippi. Among his many books, are two volumes in The Communicator's Commentary Series (Word), *Living the Psalms: A Confidence for All Seasons* (Upper Room), and workbooks on the themes of prayer and the spiritual disciplines. He currently pastors Christ United Methodist Church in Memphis, Tennessee.

Donald McCullough

It wasn't until the end of this project that Don started to get on my nerves.

When we outlined the book, he gave us thoughtful input. When he began writing, he asked pointed and wise questions to make sure he understood our audience. He turned in his chapters on time, and his work required relatively little editing.

Then it came time for him to look over our edits of his work:

"On page three, first paragraph, opening sentence," he began, "I think we need a comma after the word *ministry*."

I examined the context and had to admit he was right.

"On page six, third paragraph, second sentence," he continued, "I think *refreshes* should be singular."

Well, of course. I knew that.

"And on page eight, last line on the page, if I'm not mistaken, shouldn't there be a hyphen between *first* and *class* when it modifies a noun?"

Yeah, so? You want my job?

Our proofreaders had yet to scan the chapter, and those are the types of errors they were going to catch anyway. But it was disconcerting to have him inspect the chapters with such an eye to editorial detail!

Don approaches every task, in fact, with professionalism and attention to detail. Whether it's preaching, administration, writing — even personal growth — he devotes himself to doing the most masterful job he can.

Don is currently bringing that sense of professionalism to

Solana Beach Presbyterian Church, Solana Beach, California, as the church's senior pastor. Previously he pastored in Seattle, Washington, and he has earned a doctorate in systematic theology from the University of Edinburgh, Scotland. He has written *Waking from the American Dream* and *Finding Happiness in the Most Unlikely Places* (both InterVarsity).

Gordon MacDonald

As we sat together in his cramped Manhattan office, Gordon offered us intriguing insights into the recovery movement, the nature of evangelicalism, and the psychological dimensions of modern ministry. His mind ranged wide and deep.

For instance: "The evangelicalism I grew up in was a persuasion-oriented, crusade-oriented tradition of faith that placed tremendously high emotional expectations on people. But it only allowed us to express a very narrow band of emotions: joy, certainly, but anger, never. And we had no place for the meloncholic person, the person who perceives deeply and is troubled by the fallenness of creation. Some of the most creative people — writers, artists — are melancholic. But in the culture I grew up in, such a person could not flourish nor be creative. If you weren't joyful all the time, you weren't a real Christian."

And this: "There's a hunger built in us to hear God's approval. The very first thing God said after 'Let there be light' is an approval statement, 'It is good.' We want to hear God say about us, 'It is good,' because all of creation hungers to hear the 'well done' of the Creator.

"That's one of the reasons I believe our fathers are so important to us: they play the preliminary role of the heavenly Father when they tell us, 'Well done.' But many men haven't heard 'well done' from their fathers, and it leaves them with an almost unfillable void. They ache to have their biological father put his hand on their shoulder and say in one way or another, 'I'm just delighted with the man you are.' "

This was the same man who an hour earlier had shown a genuine pastoral interest in our waitress as she talked of weather and her job. And this was the same man who, in the midst of an unexpected eastern snowstorm, would soon insist I take his overcoat, even though he would have to do without one himself for the rest of his day.

This is Gordon MacDonald, a pastor who cares about individuals and a thinker who tries continually to grasp the significance of his life.

Gordon brings this dual passion to his work as pastor of Trinity Baptist Church in New York City. He has also pastored churches in Kansas, Illinois, and Massachusetts, and has been president of InterVarsity. He is the author of many books, including, *Restoring Your Spiritual Passion* and *Rebuilding Your Broken World*.

Each of these men has learned, sometimes through trying experiences, that his personal growth is vital to his long-term ability to minister and to minister in a way that nurtures a congregation. In *Mastering Personal Growth*, all three show how they've found time for friends and reading, for family and prayer, for ministry and retreats from ministry.

We trust you will find some insights here that will encourage you to steadily, patiently keep at this most fundamental element of a pastor's life.

— *Mark Galli*
contributing editor, LEADERSHIP
Carol Stream, Illinois

Part One
The Intentional Pastor

Nothing is nearly as powerful or more potentially beautiful than "quality of soul."

— *Gordon MacDonald*

CHAPTER ONE

What Fuels Your Growth?

It was a Saturday morning almost twenty-five years ago, and I had officiated in the burial of two homeless men during the past week. In both cases, I felt, their lives had been meaningless and wasted. I was overwhelmed with the sadness and emptiness of the experience.

Combined with several nights of inadequate sleep, no recent spiritual refreshment, and lots of nonstop ministry activity, their deaths left me in a state of emotional overload.

When I came to the breakfast table that morning, I had no clue I was on the brink of a crisis. Life had not yet prepared me for the fact that everyone has a breaking point. There at the table my point came, triggered by one innocent comment.

"You haven't spent much time with the children lately," said my wife, Gail.

She was correct. I hadn't. She had kindly avoided noting that I hadn't spent adequate time with her, either. And I hadn't done any better with my heavenly Father. Add to this that work was piling up, my sermon for the next day was unprepared, and I needed to make several hospital calls.

I felt like a baseball player who just bobbled the ball and the electronic scoreboard behind him begins to flash: ERROR! ERROR! ERROR!

Suddenly I was engulfed with a sense of futility, and I began to cry. I lost control and wept steadily for four hours. That had never happened before. It was one of a limited number of "breaking experiences" in my life, which — more than any of the so-called successes — have been most responsible for whatever growth toward quality of soul I can claim.

What happened that day forced me to face up to something I'd either ignored or wasn't smart enough to realize: I had been engaging in ministry — supposedly in the name of Jesus — largely based on natural giftedness — my ability with words, my social skills, and my desire and energy to work for long periods of time.

That Saturday morning I saw the first unavoidable results of a soul that lacked quality. Priorities were askew; key relationships were being neglected; spiritual life was a joke; work was out of control. And — I mean no silliness — ministry had ceased to be fun.

When the tears dried and I had time to assess what had happened, I saw that if I was going to persevere in ministry, I was going to have to tap deeper motivations and wellsprings of strength.

Quality of soul became the first priority. That was probably the first time I became interested in what I would later call the ordering of my private world.

Other watershed experiences have come since then — some

even more difficult to face — but this was the one that pressed me to ask the questions of motivation (what was driving me?) and maintenance (what would keep me going?).

That morning at the breakfast table caused me to get serious about issues of the spirit that I'd put on the shelf for too long. In the weeks that followed, I searched my inner world. It became a re-building effort, a reconstruction of my base for serving God in the church.

But sometimes when you begin to rebuild, you have to first clear away some rubble. Habits, motives, illusions, ambitions, and forms of pride have to be named and renounced. This activity is called repentance. I suspect it's the most powerful exercise of the inner spirit that God has given us. It's God's weapon against deceit, which, in turn, is the most powerful weapon in the arsenal of the Evil One.

I wish I could say the personal cleanup that stemmed from the Saturday morning catharsis occurred in a short time and never had to be re-addressed. But I'd speak as a fool. All that really happened was that I went on full alert to what might be the core problem of most men and women who have a heart to serve God.

It was that experience that initiated my own discipline of journaling, which I've maintained to this day. I began to discover the benefit of recording the thoughts and insights I felt God com-mending to my soul.

Searching the Motivation-Base

What I began to see in those earliest days of private-world activity was that I had to be ruthless in dealing with the motivation-base for following and serving Jesus Christ.

I'm not sure I'd ever given the root motivations in my life the attention they needed. My days in college and seminary, and even the first years in the pastorate ministry, had been colored with a sense of idealism, even glamour, about ministry. The pastor's life, I thought with a mixture of naiveté and unbounded enthusiasm, would be one of changing history, building a great church, making a difference in everyone's life, preaching with fervor to people eager to hear, and enjoying a revered position as everyone's spiritual director and mentor. And if that's what the pastor's life was, then I wanted in.

But *why* did I want in?

Few questions ascend in importance above that one. But only a sharp dose of reality — usually painful reality — will force us to look deeply at our motivations. The story of Simon the magician in Acts 8 is instructive. When this man saw Peter and others act in the power of the Holy Spirit, he was prepared to pay good money to have that ability.

I see a little of Simon's spirit in me. While I wouldn't be so brash as to pay money for the giftedness that makes ministry possible, at times I've succumbed to the temptation of paying for greater popularity and effectiveness by jeopardizing my health, sacrificing relationships, and otherwise burning myself out. I suspect that possibility exists in each of us.

Peter instantly challenged Simon's motivation-base: "You have no part or share in this ministry, because your heart is not right before God. Repent of this wickedness and pray to the Lord. Perhaps he will forgive you for having such a thought in your heart. For I see that you are full of bitterness and captive to sin" (Acts 8:21-23).

When I search my menu of motives, I find several that are not made by God. And when I've gotten into the private worlds of other colleagues, I've discovered that I'm not alone. A partial list of substandard motives might look like this:

● *The need for approval.* Paul talks a lot about our need for approval. He is unashamed to admit his desire for the approval of the "righteous judge." He is definitely out to hear God's "well done." But I'm impressed by his note to the Corinthians telling them that their approval and even his own self-approval is of no consequence to him. Only God's approval counts.

I compare myself with that standard and grow uneasy. Until I was 18, I can't remember ever considering any other profession but ministry. But the need for a wrong kind of approval may have been a major factor.

"There is no higher calling than to preach the gospel," my

mother would say to me as a child. She would add, "Now, I'm not pressuring you to do that, of course. I'd never want you to preach unless God called you to do so."

Despite her disclaimers, I interpreted the message as "Mother will be most proud and will love me most if I'm a preacher of the gospel."

Add to that a story or two I heard regularly about my days as an infant — a story, for example, about a grandmother and a mother who laid hands on my newborn body and willed my life to preaching.

Another story about two planes that collided above our home when I was 2 years old, showering our backyard with debris that should have killed me but didn't. Or a third story about my near drowning at age 3 and being rescued at the last second by someone who pulled me out of the water by my hair.

These stories, often retold, had a powerful effect upon my sense of direction. "God has protected you for a purpose," was the message mediated to me. "Find out what that intention is, and don't defy it."

I want to be respectful about the notion of God's special calling. But perhaps you can see why these experiences could become twisted into another process. Obeying God is one thing. Trying to please a mother, or wanting a father to be proud of you, is another. These motivations can get interwoven in the soul early in life. Then they get woven into the fabric of a sense of call, and it is very difficult to separate the two.

I came to see the obvious: approval from a parent or significant other can never navigate us through the often stormy waters of ministry. If we are driven by the need to hear the "well done" from human beings, even parents, we get maneuvered into something like an addiction. A certain amount of approval needed this year will, like a drug, need to be increased next year. We wind up needing more and more approval as time passes to keep up the same drive.

And since people's approval inevitably comes and goes, increases and evaporates, motivation through approval becomes a yo-yo of emotions. It's one of the first reasons men and women quit spiritual leadership. No one's clapping anymore.

Want a contrast to Simon and his evil motives? It's John the Baptist, who one day watched a formerly approving crowd leave him to follow Jesus. His reaction? "I must decrease." Only a person free of the need for approval could talk like that.

● *The validation from achievement.* Most of us have grown up in a system highly influenced by the ethic of achievement. And the message seems clear: those who are successful have been clearly visited with the hand of God. The corollary is likewise clear: those who are wildly successful — more so than others — have been visited with the *special* hand of God.

Success is usually measured in the founding or the developing of great institutions or large followings. In evangelism, it means drawing the largest crowds. In church leadership, it means heading the largest church in the region. In other ministries, it means leading the fastest growing organization (in terms of income, staff, and influence). In the publishing world, it means producing the best sellers.

When we hear Christians praise these "winners," many of us are tempted to hear that "my value" will be substantiated only when I am equally successful. And if I am not hearing this kind of praise, then perhaps I am not as valuable to God as I was meant to be.

Perhaps the most dramatic statement of achievement motivation was what reputedly was said to evangelist D. L. Moody (and countless others): "The world has yet to see what God can do with one man who is totally yielded to his will."

I know many bewildered men and women who have tried their hardest to fulfill the spirit of that statement. They set out to serve God believing they are totally "yielded." But neither they nor the world ever saw any great results. They thus live in perpetual disillusionment, wondering why their faith, their labor, their commitment was not good enough to produce the results others have gained.

I recall the words of a chapel speaker during my seminary days who confused us by saying, "Don't aspire to high leadership unless it is thrust upon you." At the time that didn't make sense to me, especially since we students were constantly being told in subtle (and not so subtle) ways that the successful leader is clearly a person upon whom God's pleasure rests.

So I, like others, fantasized about pastoring a large church. And by the time I was in my mid-thirties, I'd been "blessed" with the fulfillment of that dream. But then I knew what the chapel speaker meant: there is little joy or prolonged satisfaction in high leadership if achievement is your motivation.

I discovered in those days that leadership made physical, spiritual, and emotional demands that I'd never anticipated. And without a disciplined spirit, I simply wouldn't have the reserves to go the distance. It's possible that our seminary professors told us that, but if they did, a lot of us didn't get the message. Apparently every generation has to learn the lesson the same way — the hard way.

The Bible gives us a lot of disproportionate insights. Think, for example, of all the pages devoted to the championship performances of Paul and Daniel and Moses and Esther. One evangelized his world; another served three kings with honor and bravery; a third built a nation; a fourth rescued her generation from a holocaust.

Then one reads of another, Enoch, of whom it is simply said, "(He) walked with God; then he was no more, because God took him away." Not much detail; no accolades; no achievements of record. But one nevertheless gets the feeling that Enoch is the equal of all the others, if not their superior.

• *The longing for intimacy.* Those who study temperament styles of people know that a certain percentage of the population is driven by intimacy: the desire to connect closely with people.

There are some who love to make things or draw things or throw things or think about things. But men and women in ministry are usually disinterested in things. They're drawn to people. They want to understand them, motivate them, encourage them, and probably, change them.

Put them into a room of people, and ministry people are suddenly feeling all the pain, the possibilities, the problems, and passions that are there. And they want to connect with it all, bringing meaning or healing or modification to it. That, in good measure, is the typical pastoral temperament.

The pastoral life offers great opportunity to the person who enjoys intimacy with other human beings. Properly directed, it is one of the most powerful gifts there is. Improperly directed, it leads to manipulation, exploitation, and sexual sin.

If one has entered the ministry simply because it is a wonderful place to meet one's need for people-connection, the results are likely to be disastrous.

I've heard more than a few midlife men talk about leaving their careers in the marketplace to enter ministry. They're prepared to shelve a work history of twenty years to go to seminary and become a pastor. Why? Because most of the time they're disillusioned making and selling widgets; they hate the depersonalization of the marketplace; they long to stop being so lonely and to get close to people. They observe pastors, who appear to spend all day talking with folks, solving problems, leading and motivating, and it looks good to them.

Scan the motive-base and you usually see that the primary caller to ministry may not be Christ but rather a need to assuage the sense of isolation and alienation that careerism has created.

Timothy could have been driven by this desire for intimacy. You get the feeling he liked to make people feel good. And that's why Paul has to push him to preach, to confront, to prod, to stay the course: "Remember the gift that's in you." Without Paul's challenges, Timothy possibly would have settled down to being an awfully nice guy.

● *The power of idealism*. I grew up in a highly idealistic tradition. I was immersed in triumphal language. We were going to "convert the nations" and "win the world for Christ." My early heroes were spiritual giants (at least their biographers depicted them as giants) such as Hudson Taylor and George Mueller. And my generation of Christian leaders attached an almost mystical dimension to their calling. Paul's words — "Woe to me if I do not preach the Gospel" — rested heavily upon us. More than once I heard, "If God has given you a call and you forsake that call for anything else, you're going to live in life-long judgment."

When I first entered ministry as a youth pastor, I was filled with that idealism. I remember my first sermon and how Gail hugged me so tightly at the end of the evening. She was proud of me; I was proud of me. We saw only a wonderful future of doing God's work.

Then a few months later the sky began to fall. The father of one of the young people became disaffected by how I handled his son. He wrote me a letter saying I should go into the army; it would make a man out of me. My idealism crashed that day. It was one of the first times I realized that doing God's work, even with my best intentions, wasn't always going to be pleasant.

A few months later, I picked up a crumpled piece of paper and read a note one teenager had written to another: "If MacDonald doesn't leave here pretty soon, this whole program is going to die."

I was so discouraged that I wrote my letter of resignation and quit. I spent the next year working nights, typing bills for a trucking company. All the dreams and expectations were gone. There was no idealism during those months.

What I had to learn was that ministry is hard work — a noble work but hard. And it is marked with failures and disappointments, with opposition and misunderstanding. No one had succeeded in acquainting me with Paul's momentary crashes: "We were so utterly, unbearably crushed that we despaired of life itself."

There is probably no such thing as a pure motivation. Frankly, our hearts have too much evil embedded in them. And I suspect that even the motivations originating somewhere near purity are likely to be perverted as time goes by.

Many find it easy to write off high-profile Christians who have experienced stunning failures of one kind or another. There may be some exceptions, but I am convinced that almost every one of those who have built reputations and have collapsed started with the best of motivations. They really wanted to serve God. But the best of motivations are exchangeable for less-than-best.

Only the man or woman who *baptizes* his or her motivations

every day will have any hope that things will not turn sour down the road.

I don't know why anyone ever wanted the job of an Old Testament prophet — indeed many of those who got the job weren't seeking it. Jeremiah is a case in point. He fights the call when it comes: "I can't speak; I'm a child." Later on he confesses that he'd like to run from the city and seclude himself in the countryside (I can identify with that). Jeremiah and others prompt me to think that there is some safety when you find yourself kicking against God's call every once in a while. When you do kick, the motive-base gets a re-testing.

These sample motivations that I've tried to list and describe are fairly typical of the things likely to drive us in our younger years. But time and struggle are likely to force impurities to the surface. And each time that happens, we have to decide all over again if we will purify our motives before God and other people, or, as an alternative, grow increasingly cynical about why we entered ministry in the first place.

Many men and women reach their midlife and discover their motivations for ministry are inadequate. They think it's too late to change. And so they continue on. They work their hardest to fulfill the expectations of their jobs. But that's all they're likely to be doing: jobs — nice jobs, helpful jobs, honorable jobs, but jobs.

By the time you reach your fifties, you may have had a number of rebuilding efforts. They usually come as a result of setbacks. Here perhaps is the one place I can safely boast (as Paul did in his weaknesses). I have known several of the classic setbacks. And, as a result, I've come to learn something about restorative grace and the process of rebuilding.

Are there great and noble motives? Of course. Moses became absorbed in the suffering of his people, and God's sensitivity to suffering and bondage became his. Samuel came to understand that the people of Israel were unable to hear God's voice through the present religious establishment. He made his voice available to God. Mary, the mother of the Lord, was clearly driven by the principle of obedience and allowed herself to be the mother of the Lamb of God.

These are the motives we can nourish in our own lives.

Motives Are Never Fixed

Is it healthy to be concerned about our motive-base? Well, Peter did it with Simon the magician; I see the prophets wrestling with it. And I see Jesus reflecting upon his motive-base every time he reiterates his sense of call from the Father.

Perhaps it's a function of the older years that makes one more and more wary. I now realize that the best of motives and attitudes can be twisted even after we think we've gotten them straight.

In 1981 I went to Thailand to attend a congress of evangelical leaders. I was given the honor of delivering one of the plenary addresses. I remember thinking, *Wow! Here are hundreds of Christian leaders from scores of countries, and I am one of the very, very few asked to give a talk to the whole assembly.*

It started as a heady time, and I remember having to rethink my motives with regularity. The drive to achieve (hadn't I proved myself?), to find approval (wouldn't my mother be proud?), to connect (these people must like me), and to realize leadership goals (being a part of a world leadership was sort of an objective) were all at work. I had a lot of soul scanning and confessing to do.

Then three days into the conference, one of the most well-known leaders chartered a boat and invited about forty of the conferees for an afternoon of quiet consultation out on the Gulf of Siam. They were going to talk about the future of evangelical Christianity in the world. I was not among the forty.

Suddenly being one of the speakers at the conference meant nothing. I was devastated. Not being invited to that meeting on the boat left me feeling empty. And God taught me one of the most important lessons of my life: no matter how far you go or how high you think you've climbed, there will always be forty (and probably many, many more) above and beyond you.

The moment you think of the kingdom as a place to achieve, to become valuable, to connect, or to be a major player, you will quickly discover that this was never what Jesus had in mind when he called, "Follow me."

In my book *Rebuilding Your Broken World*, I recount the story of Alexander Whyte, the great Scottish preacher, who was told that an American evangelist had accused a close friend of his of not being a converted man. Whyte was instantly outraged. His speech was barely restrained as he vented his fury on his friend's accuser.

But then, when Whyte quieted down, he was told that the same evangelist had also questioned Whyte's conversion. Instantly, Whyte fell silent. Now there was no rebuttal, just an awful quietness as he buried his face in his hands. Then he looked up at the one who had brought these reports and said, "Leave me. Leave me, my friend. I must examine my heart."

I don't think there's a person in this world who remembers what I said in my speech in Thailand. It wasn't that good anyway. But I will always value that trip. There I, like Whyte, learned an important lesson: Examine your heart. Make sure you know which motivations are in control, and don't dare step into public until you've got the answer.

At the heart of ministry is the heart, a heart close to God.
— Maxie Dunnam

CHAPTER TWO

Cultivating Closeness with God

A fter I finished seminary in the late 1950s, I organized a new church in Gulfport, Mississippi. From a church growth perspective, it was a huge success. With rapid growth, a new building, and suburban prosperity, the church was the Cinderella of our conference.

But increasingly I was miserable. I felt like an organization man, not a man of God. I wasn't taking my directions from the Lord. In the midst of a thriving church setting, I felt far from God. For a while I thought seriously about leaving the ministry.

In retrospect, I see I was running on my own power, relying on my own resources. But I didn't know how to do otherwise. There was no question about my commitment to Christ or my call to preach. It was a matter of power, spiritual power: the inner resources for living with a strength not my own. Seminaries at the time didn't offer help on spiritual formation. In short, my relationship with God was hardly more than a formality.

Few things are as hollow as a relationship intended for passion that instead is marked by mere duty. When the heat of a couple's romance and honeymoon is cooled by concerns over mortgage payments, child raising, and household chores, the relationship becomes drudgery: husband and wife don't kiss each other at the door; they make love as if it were a mere routine; they stare past their dinner plates with nothing to talk about.

So it is in ministry. A love relationship, which is what God intends us to have with him, is necessary for a vital ministry. At the heart of ministry is the heart, a heart close to God.

Being Close Is More than a Feeling

While serving the church in Mississippi, my spiritual rebuilding began. And years later, after walking diligently on a pilgrimage of spiritual growth, I found myself with another dilemma — and an opportunity to get closer to God.

I was in California at the time, pastoring another church. I was increasingly getting invitations from across the country to lead conferences and retreats on the subject of spirituality. Then I received two invitations, each to join a parachurch ministry, one as the leader of a retreat center and the other as a staff member of a mission organization. I found myself extremely perplexed: should I remain in pastoral ministry or move into parachurch service? Since this occurred at a critical juncture in my career, I knew I was asking a most fundamental question: What should I do with the rest of my life?

To help with my decision, I took a retreat to pray and find direction. By this time I had made up my mind to accept a position with one of the two parachurch organizations. I went to the mountains simply to decide which one. The result was as dramatic as my conversion experience: I felt the Lord telling me to stay put, to remain a pastor. With as much confidence as I've had about anything, I refused both invitations and continued pastoring the California church.

In that period, I felt as close to God and as centered in his will as I've ever felt. It illustrates what it means to me to be close to God: at the core, it means having an internal sense of harmony with what God wants me to do.

Early in my spiritual journey (and to some degree now), I depended on the feeling of God's nearness. Though feelings are wonderful and beneficial, I don't want to rely on them. Instead of considering how I feel at the moment, I try to discern how centered I am in God's leading.

For example, in Memphis we recently elected our first black mayor. Unfortunately people voted along racial lines, Memphis being 52 percent black. To help unify our city, I felt the white community needed to show our support for our newly elected mayor. So I persuaded the pastors of some of the largest white churches in town to pay for and sign an open letter of support in the local newspaper.

We took some heat for doing that. A few members resigned from my congregation, and the mail and calls from outside were pretty tough. That dampened my emotions. Frankly, I didn't feel particularly close to the Lord at the time. I knew, however, I was doing what was right. That certainty assured me that I was with God even though I did not feel close to him.

Even when I don't know God's will, if I'm at least seeking it earnestly, that is enough. A man and woman who struggle to "get on the same page" often feel closer after they've worked through their difficulties. Waiting on God does the same for me.

I identify with a friend who, after being asked to consider becoming a candidate for bishop in the Methodist church, said, "I'm in the middle of that decision right now, and I'm not getting any direction, but I'm feeling close to the Lord because I'm struggling, I'm dependent. I feel in resonance with the Spirit; while I don't have an answer, I'm where God wants me to be because I'm focused on him."

Warning Signs of a Distance Problem

If feeling close to God is not a sure indicator of one's closeness, neither is a feeling of distance to be equated with a poor relationship with God. So I must have some other signs that signal how I am with God. Here are a few I find helpful:

● *I have no heart for ministry.* This is key for me. In fact, I'm more concerned about losing my appetite for ministry than I am about burnout; loss of heart can be so spiritually deceptive.

A pastor who has lost his or her appetite functions in the system, performs well in the local church, does everything required with finesse and professional skill, succeeds at keeping the church going. But there's no excitement. There's no sitting on the edge of one's seat to share something great God has done recently in one's own life or in the congregation. Furthermore, there's no heart for doing the hard thing and no burning concern for missions or outreach, unless the church rolls start to suffer.

The void in the pastor's heart may not even be perceived and certainly not confessed. My church members in Mississippi thought everything was tremendous — after all, we were the fastest growing church in the local Methodist conference. Because the church was doing well, they thought I was doing well. With all the "success" surrounding me, I was tempted sometimes to ignore my inner warning signals and assume that was as good as ministry was going to get.

Although this is perhaps the largest and brightest warning light we should notice, others less ominous are worthy of our attention.

● *I feel depressed about my spirituality for a significant period of time.* Recently I was confronted with a major decision about the course of my ministry. Although I spent extended time daily in prayer and Scripture reading, for two months I was unable to sense any direction from God. I finally got to the point where I was simply numb, unable to progress in my thinking about the decision. I knew then that something was wrong.

● *My decisions are not thought through.* In this regard, my wife serves as a barometer of my relationship with God. She has an uncanny way of asking the questions that show that I've not given enough thought and prayer to a decision. She also shows me how I take a simple decision and complicate it, sometimes because I'm seeking to evade God's way of doing something.

● *My emotions are off base, inappropriate.* I've discovered that the way I respond to telephone calls can be a signal. When I begin thinking, *Oh no, another phone call,* or start procrastinating returning calls, it's time to stop and assess what's going on. It's likely that I no longer have the spiritual resources to meet the demands of my calling.

● *I have a chronic problem with sleeplessness.* Sometimes sleeplessness is of God. I have been awakened by God to receive some message that I haven't received during my working day. Some of my most meaningful times of prayer and spiritual reflection have come in the early hours of the morning.

But chronic sleeplessness is often a sign that I'm not only overworked but also working on my own steam, not depending on God's power.

One recent month was particularly hectic. I spent ten days in Russia, followed by three days at home — one of them a Sunday with full preaching responsibilities — and then two weeks in a demanding denominational meeting. Though in the weeks following I had time to recover physically, I was still waking up in the middle of the night. That signaled that busyness had affected me spiritually.

Making the Most of the Pastoral Role

Just as marriage can both enhance and detract from the romantic passion between a man and woman, so the pastoral role is both a boon and a bane to spirituality. We are wise to be alert to its possibilities.

Being a pastor hinders closeness to God in several ways:

● *Busyness.* Shopkeeping chores, as Eugene Peterson so aptly describes church administrative tasks, and constant interaction with people, all to keep an organization humming, take time, attention, and enormous amounts of energy. That often leaves us little concentrated time with God.

If we do attend to the spiritual disciplines in such a ministry, we often do so less because we desire closeness with God and more because we are supposed to: it's our job, all duty and no delight. We can conduct spiritual disciplines like a factory worker punches the clock. We pursue spirituality as a military man pursues stripes on his uniform.

• *The professional side to ministry.* Pastors, in order to do their jobs well, need to learn certain professional skills: how to conduct meetings, how to be diplomatic in all kinds of situations, how to juggle family and ministry, how and when to take community responsibilities.

In addition, if one seeks to expand one's ministry by serving larger and larger parishes and provide increased security for one's family, you have to build relationships in the denomination and, most likely, attain another advanced degree.

In the process of jumping through all the hoops toward becoming a "professional," though, we may begin losing our passion for prayer. Although no one makes a deliberate decision to eliminate prayer or to stop depending on the Holy Spirit, walking on the path of pastoral professionalism has a way of making us feel less dependent on God.

• *Scheduling freedom.* Pastors, more than most professionals, have the ability to set their own schedules. Except for Sunday morning worship and the monthly board meeting, our time is pretty much ours to manage.

In some church settings, if we are content to do so, a pastor can cover the required bases without working especially hard. Pastoral ministry can be the most demanding work or the most cushy work on earth, depending on what we make of it.

• *Lots of affirmation.* When we do our jobs well, especially when we respond with compassion to our people, they will affirm us lavishly. But the amazing thing is we often don't have to do well for people to praise us. No matter how poorly we do, in fact, there are always some kindhearted souls in the congregation who will tell us we're doing great.

Whether the praise is due or not, if we hear enough of it, we may assume that we're God's person, that all is well with us, when nothing could be further from the truth.

● *Regular contact with the sacred.* Whether it's leading a Bible study or preaching a sermon, opening a meeting in prayer or closing worship with a benediction, baptizing people or serving communion, we're constantly handling holy things. But continual absorption in spiritual things breeds a dullness toward the sacred. Unless we are humble and pay full attention to what we are saying and doing, the holy can become routine, and that can lead to a spiritual dullness that is hard to sharpen.

Fortunately these spiritual hazards are balanced by the unique opportunities ministry offers to the spiritual life.

● *We are regularly confronted with our need for God.* My daughter is a hospital chaplain. She became well-acquainted with an elderly woman who was a cancer patient. One day my daughter went into her room and sensed she was near death.

At a loss as to what to do, she sat beside the woman's bed and prayed silently for her. Almost unconsciously she began to caress the woman's hair. After a while she started singing to her, singing an old lullaby my wife and I sang to our children when putting them to bed.

In the middle of her singing, my daughter felt a presence in the room and assumed someone had come in the room behind her. She was embarrassed about her singing and hesitated to turn around, but when she did, nobody was there. Kim quickly realized she had sensed the presence of Christ.

Such life and death situations, in which human limitations are so apparent, remind us of our utter dependence on God and our need for prayer.

● *Constant contact with the holy.* This, as I mentioned, can be a challenge, but it is also a blessing when approached in the right attitude. For me that means humility.

Take my preaching, for instance, an opportunity to exegete God's Word and proclaim it to others. To keep this holy event from becoming routine, I'm intentional about revealing my shortcomings and concerns from the pulpit. I have found that if publicly I'm fairly vulnerable about my shortcomings and my desires to walk more fully in God's will, that puts demands on me to follow through.

If, for instance, I admit in the pulpit that I need to spend more time in prayer and that I have made plans on how to improve, I feel accountable to the congregation to pray more.

• *Interaction with "saints."* I regularly call on several people in our church for prayer and advice; I especially value their spiritual insights and discernment.

One is an older woman with a vocation of intercession. Another is a young couple with a special freshness about their faith. In many ways I look to these people as models of spiritual maturity. In my role as pastor I am privileged to speak with such people often, and that encourages my spirituality.

Getting Closer

I have found six things especially helpful in keeping me close to God. Granted, we are each different when it comes to spirituality, but here is what has worked for me.

• *Attend to the emotional.* Pastors can be hindered spiritually by their emotions and personalities. For example, when I first moved to California, I became increasingly insecure about myself. Having been raised in poverty, I felt I lacked education and sufficient exposure to the finer things of life. I felt inferior to others, and that hampered me both emotionally and spiritually.

Eventually, I sought a professional counselor and attended a therapy group, which turned things around for me. Getting my emotions straightened out really helped me spiritually: I was able, for instance, to accept God's acceptance of me, no matter my background, and that freed me to start using the gifts I did have for his service.

• *Practice spiritual disciplines.* I often find it helpful to hear how others do this so that I can fine tune my approach. Here's my procedure:

I get up at 6 A.M., put on a pot of coffee (the first discipline!), and go to my study, which is in my home. I begin with intercession. Devotional reading follows; often I use a devotional guide along with the Scriptures. Then I spend time in reflection, pondering what I've read, examining my life, listening to the Lord.

Naturally, sometimes this morning time is tremendously rewarding and exciting, with things popping off the page and insights coming left and right. At other times it's dry and seemingly fruitless. But overall, it's worked for me.

• *Retreats*. I schedule two personal retreats a year as "regular maintenance" for my soul, one around my birthday, and another, about six months later.

In addition, I sometimes need an unscheduled time away to break through a prolonged dry period. Short retreats of one day are usually sufficient.

• *Practice the presence*. When I don't feel God's presence, I've learned the importance of practicing God's presence. For me this most often means sharing God's presence — his love and goodness — with someone else.

Recently a woman in our church was admitted to the Mayo Clinic to await a liver transplant. I wanted to convey the presence of God to her, but I hesitated at first because at the time I wasn't feeling God's presence in my own life. I didn't want to sound artificial to her.

But I decided not to wait until I was "in the mood," and I deliberately phoned her to assure her of God's presence in her situation. I practiced God's presence by reaching out to someone else.

John Wesley encouraged Christians to practice "acts of mercy" partly because in many ways we act our way into Christlikeness more than we pray, study, or worship our way into Christlikeness.

• *Keep stretched*. After preaching and administrating a church for a few years, I face the danger of feeling I'm in control, that I can, through mere technique, bring about effectiveness and success. To counteract that, I welcome ministries that push me out of my control zone.

On Sunday nights our church holds healing services, where we partake of Communion, anoint people with oil, and pray for them. It's something that has not been usual in my tradition, so I'm on a learning curve as to how to minister through it effectively. Besides, when praying for the sick, I can't feel anything but dependent on God.

● *Nurture relationships.* John Wesley used the term *conferencing* to describe intentional reflection and sharing with others about what God is doing in your life. The most important person with whom I do this is my wife, but I also conference regularly with others.

Two questions I find helpful when meeting with others are: (1) When this week did you feel closest to God? and (2) When did you have a discipleship opportunity, the chance to experience growth yourself or to help others grow, but ignored it? The first question leads to a greater awareness of our experience and relationship with God, and the second sensitizes us to opportunities for growth.

Once in a while I ask my family and fellow workers what, in their view, is going well with me and what things should I be cautioned about.

Especially when I'm making decisions about God's direction for my life, consulting others helps me accurately hear from God. With big decisions, I can easily get sidetracked by my emotions and desires.

In the throes of one major decision, I called a friend and during our conversation asked, "Do you think I'll be happy if I do this?"

"You don't have any right to ask that question," he replied.

That shocked me. But the more I thought about it, the more I saw his point; the question was not happiness but rather fruitfulness and meaning and obedience. I needed to hear that.

I'm happy when the church I serve grows, when ministry expands, when what I do is "successful." But I've learned to see that as secondary. What really sustains my life and ministry is God, and the closer I am to him, the more fruitful and satisfying is my work for him.

Part Two
Sustaining Relationships

When we consider the blessings of God — the gifts that add beauty and joy to our lives, that enable us to keep going through stretches of boredom and even suffering — friendship is very near the top.
— *Donald McCullough*

CHAPTER THREE

Friends for the One at the Top

A few years back Pepper Rogers had a terrible season as football coach at UCLA. It even upset his home life. "My dog was my only friend," he recalls. "I told my wife that a man needs at least two friends, and she bought me another dog."

More than a few pastors can identify too closely with this story; some have already started stockpiling Alpo.

I haven't taken a scientific poll, but as I speak with colleagues in ministry, I've come to believe loneliness afflicts clergy like a cloud of locusts in Pharaoh's Egypt. Many of us, no doubt, would agree with nineteenth century German philosopher Arthur Schopenhauer that friendship belongs in the same class as sea serpents — something conjectured but not yet proven. Having a friend who, as the Bible says, sticks closer than a brother seems about as likely as spotting the Loch Ness Monster.

Yet when we consider the blessings of God — the gifts that add beauty and joy to our lives, that enable us to keep going through stretches of boredom and even suffering — friendship is very near the top. Perhaps Gordon Liddy can say (upon being released from prison), "I have found within myself all I need and all I ever shall need," but the rest of us do not envy him. Who wants to be completely alone?

We use the word *friend* in different ways. "Dear friends in Christ," we address the congregational letter; or "I want you to meet my friend," we say, referring to someone we have been with only a couple of times; or "My friend is dying of cancer," we choke up, knowing that when he dies a part of us will die too. There are different levels of friendship.

Pastors usually have plenty of people with whom they can wade around in the shallow waters of friendship; they work together on church committees, they socialize once or twice a year, they readily refer to each other as friends. But this chapter will focus on those we call *good* friends or *best* friends, those with whom we share the adventure of sailing out into the deep waters of friendship.

The Risks of Loneliness

Before exploring the dynamics of friendship, we do well to ponder the heavy toll that lack of friendship can take on us.

Loneliness is lousy. It adds one more emotional burden to the already heavy load of a shepherd, who has to look after an unruly flock of critters who seem forever dedicated to wandering away, getting caught in wire fences, and finding themselves stranded on dangerous precipices. A shepherd needs to be as emotionally fit as possible for the rigorous tasks of ministry.

Even more important, loneliness distorts reality. Sometimes

we find ourselves caught between two problems: insecurity and arrogance. We are in positions where being liked by others bears significantly on our success, and thus we inevitably worry about our approval rating. To compensate for feelings of insecurity, a pastor may project an image of faultless competence, an image of self-assured control. And insecurity and arrogance coupled with loneliness are like sticks of dynamite ready to explode.

Without friends a low self-esteem gets beaten down even lower. *If I have no friends,* I begin to think, *I must be unfriendly. If no one loves me, I must be unlovable.* Loneliness and insecurity interact in a downward spiral of emotional death.

Furthermore, without friends we don't have the necessary counterweight to arrogance. When you're not too sure about yourself anyway, it's tempting to grasp eagerly at every affirmation that comes your way. Before long you start believing it all; you really must be extraordinary if this many people think you're hot stuff.

Good friends have a way of keeping our feet on the ground. They've seen us throw tantrums on the tennis court; they've seen us snap at our kids; they know and can remind us that there's an ordinary person living under the pulpit robe.

Pastors need friends. There may be risks whenever pastors get close to people, but we were never called to a risk-free life! We were called to follow Jesus Christ. The model for our shepherding is the Great Shepherd himself. Without doubt, he had friends: Peter, James, and John in particular.

According to John's account of their last evening together, Jesus told his disciples: "This is my commandment, that you love one another as I have loved you. No one has greater love than this, to lay down one's life for one's friends. You are my friends if you do what I command you. I do not call you servants any longer, because the servant does not know what the master is doing, but I have called you friends, because I have made known to you everything that I have heard from my Father. You did not choose me, but I chose you. And I appointed you to go and bear fruit, fruit that will last, so that the Father will give you whatever you ask in my name. I am giving you these commands so that you may love one another" (John 15:12–17, NRSV).

Taking the Initiative

"You did not choose me," Jesus told his friends, "but I chose you." Jesus built relationships by taking the initiative.

Peter, Andrew, James, and John were busy with their work: mending nets, worrying about making payments on their boats, swapping stories heard in the market, arguing about the weather. Into their world Jesus went and said, "Come, follow me."

Matthew was sitting in the tax office, spending his time between balance sheets and friends you wouldn't take home to meet your mother. Into his world Jesus went and said, "Come, follow me." Jesus invited others to share his life in a special way.

We see this same assertiveness in Barnabas, who had the courage to extend the right hand of fellowship to a notorious hater of Christ's disciples named Paul. And Paul himself, while preaching in Asia Minor, spotted Timothy, a young man with potential for ministry, and invited him to join his adventure.

Some friendships, of course, seem to happen by accident. You're at a concert, say, and in the few minutes before curtain time, you introduce yourself to the man seated next to you. He asks what you do for a living. When you tell him, he laughs. He too pastors a church, on the other side of town. Coffee and conversation after the concert begins a wonderful friendship. It sometimes happens this way.

But usually those in leadership must expect to shoulder the burden of beginning a relationship. If a friendship develops, it's because they've taken the initiative to make it possible. Leaders are generally kept at a distance; those around them don't want to be presumptuous.

I've noticed people assume a great deal about me because I'm a pastor: they assume that I'm always busy, that I have many friends, that I would prefer more interesting company.

"Pastor, we've been meaning to have you over for dinner," they say, "but we know how busy you are." And unless my experience is unique, the larger the church, the more readily people make these assumptions. So pastors need to enter the world of fishing boats and tax offices to begin developing friendships.

But we should be cautious: we can be too aggressive. Holding an office of authority, we can muscle our way into the lives of others. Human beings, though, are complex, mysterious, and "mystery withers at the touch of force." Friendship, like a dance, may require someone to take the lead, but both partners must move with the music.

Making Time for Friends

The pastors I know feel pulled in too many directions. How can anyone fulfill the impossible job description of spiritual director, preacher, counselor, administrator, fund raiser, marry-er, bury-er, and raconteur at women's association teas? There just doesn't seem to be enough time. Something must give — and what usually gives is the pastor's personal life.

Developing a friendship almost seems, well, selfish. But if the risks in not having friends are greater than the risks in having them, we have little choice.

For the sake of personal health and for the sake of the ministry itself, I schedule occasions for friendships to develop.

● *Weekly breakfasts or lunches.* For years I have been committed to having breakfast with Ken Regan every Wednesday at 6:30 A.M. We meet that early because neither of us can afford to get to our offices any later. One hour a week doesn't seem like much, but over a period of years it adds up.

● *Denominational meetings.* Denominational meetings would send me into a Twilight Zone of mental aberration, making me a danger to myself and others — if it wasn't for Woody Garvin. My mood changes the moment I see him enter the monthly Presbytery meeting. We reward ourselves for enduring the tedium of these meetings by having dinner together. Others may think we're being clubby, exclusive, but we've nurtured a good friendship because of it.

And the annual trip to our General Assembly becomes a rich opportunity for spending time with Woody. By rooming together, we not only save our churches' money, we give ourselves plenty of time to talk.

● *Study leaves.* Study leaves can be another opportunity for scheduling time with a friend. Last year Woody and I went to the Lyman Beecher lectures at Yale Divinity School. The content of the convocation was worthwhile; the best part of the week, however, was the time we spent together, the conversations and adventures shared.

Friendship with Whom?

Finding time for deep-water friendships may be easier than finding someone compatible for friendship. Here are the groups from which I have met friends:

● *Other shepherds.* Blessed is the pastor who has another pastor as a good friend. When United Airlines Flight 232 crashed just short of the landing strip in Sioux City, Iowa, on July 19, 1989, 120 people were killed. Passenger Jerry Schemmel is involved with a support group organized to help the 184 survivors cope with the lingering emotional trauma.

Wire services quoted him as saying, "For me, talking to other survivors is probably the most valuable thing, as far as therapy. . . . You can talk to counselors, your wife, your family, but when you sit down in front of another person who went through the same thing you did, you know that person relates exactly to what you're talking about."

Other pastors know exactly what we're going through: they've had troubles with the staff, known the exhilaration of Sunday morning, and written unsent letters of resignation after board meetings. We speak the common language of shared experience.

● *The sheep in your flock.* Voices from our past whisper that pastors shouldn't have friends, especially close friends, within their congregations. The old advice seems wise. We certainly want to avoid the accusation of favoritism. We also know our friends in the congregation may go through problems and suddenly need a pastor with authority. It might be difficult for them to seek marriage counseling from someone they've just observed bickering with his wife, or to seek financial counseling from someone who trounced them in

Monopoly last Friday night.

Once my family spent a week camping with another family in the church. The following Sunday the wife greeted me with a formal handshake and said, "Hello, Pastor." We had just spent a week eating at the same picnic table, sitting around the same campfire, sharing the same mosquito repellent, but she couldn't bring herself to say, "Hello, Don." She wanted me to know that I was still her pastor.

I was a bit hurt, but I understood. Many parishioners want their pastor, if not on a pedestal, at least at some distance.

Unless we nurture congregational friendship, though, we will likely remain lonely. Most of us have little opportunity to cultivate relationships outside the congregation; we must draw upon this source. Still I try to adhere to two cautions.

First, I don't hurry. There is no real friendship without trust. Before sailing out into the relational depths, I poke and probe the other's character: Will he keep a secret? Will she graciously sift through the chaff of my depressed days? Will he know what's appropriate when he tells stories about me? Will she provide wise counsel?

Second, I don't flaunt it. You shouldn't have to hide your friendships, but neither should your congregation have to deal needlessly with feelings of jealousy. So I steer clear of close friends in congregational settings; I am everyone's pastor and official "friend" on those occasions. Though I have breakfast every week with Ken Regan, on Sunday mornings I rarely even wave to him.

● *The opposite sex.* I am hesitant to rule out half the human race as a source of potential friends. A man and woman can be "just friends," I believe, to the mutual enrichment of both. I am grateful for my friendships with women; they add a dimension to my life that could not be supplied by men.

But I must nevertheless register a strong word of caution: we are sexual creatures (praise God!) and thus always vulnerable to the delights of the erotic.

While this danger does not automatically rule out male/female friendships, it does set up warning flags we dare not ignore. We ought to cultivate deep friendships with the opposite sex in the same way we would take up hang gliding or rock climbing: *very* carefully.

Alan Loy McGinnis, in his book, *The Friendship Factor*, lists ways to keep sexual feelings under control in male/female friendships: (1) Don't trust yourself too far. (2) Select companions who have strong marriages themselves. (3) Be sensible about when and where you meet alone. (4) Talk to your mate about your friendships. (5) Draw a line for physical contact. (6) Bail out if necessary.

Friendships with the opposite sex call for a good deal of common (or perhaps uncommon) sense.

Revealing Yourself

Selecting those with whom we'll cultivate relationships may be the first step toward friendship, but before we can travel further down the road, we must risk transparency. Jesus' statement to his disciples points us in the right direction:

"I have called you friends," Jesus confides in them, "because I have made known to you everything that I have heard from my Father."

Jesus' self-disclosure to his disciples lifted them to the status of friends, providing us with another principle from Jesus' ministry: If you want close friends, you must open yourself to others. The deepest friendships emerge only when the barriers have been dropped, only when the masks have been removed.

A time comes, if you want the relationship to grow, when you must risk self-disclosure. This usually happens gradually. The protective barrier we've erected around ourselves isn't razed with one blast of explosive honesty; it's taken down plank by plank.

Questions may race through our minds when we're about to reveal a hidden part of ourselves: *Will he keep this confidence? Will he reject me if he knows this about me?* But eventually the wall must fall so the other person can enter our lives.

This isn't easy for pastors. We expend much psychic energy in the creation of a public persona we wear most of the time. It doesn't matter whether I'm shopping in a supermarket or running along the beach or browsing in a bookstore: people stop me, introduce themselves as members of my church, and want to talk.

I moan to my wife, "I have to be good all the time." What I'm really saying, of course, is that I have to be pastor all the time. It's as though the persona has been fastened to me with *Super Glue.*

But we need to take off the mask for our close friends. Self-disclosure takes time and requires patience. It always seeks the balance between revelation and concealment. Jesus didn't tell the disciples everything on their first day together. It took two years before he even asked them who they thought he was; it took three years before he called them friends.

This is why old friends tend to be best friends. We've covered some distance together; we've been through stormy seas and endured the boredom of windless days; we've run aground a few times; perhaps we've even stayed as far away from each other as the ship would allow. But in sailing together, year after year, we've come to know each other well.

Twenty years ago Woody and I were in seminary. I was prodding him to learn the declensions of the Greek verbs; he was pushing me to join him in demonstrations against the war. Since then we've shared good times and bad, investing in each other and the relationship, and now we have a pretty fat account on which to draw.

We also have enough stories to get each other run out of most of the churches in America. But I will never tell, and neither will he. That's why recently I didn't think twice about calling him with a personal problem, even though it was his sermon preparation day and his secretary would need to put her life on the line to interrupt him. A relationship like this doesn't happen overnight.

Sacrificing Yourself

Initiating relationships and revealing ourselves will take us a long way toward deep friendship. But we're not there yet. Jesus, in word and action, showed one more important element. "No one has greater love than this," he said, "to lay down one's life for one's friends." By the time these words were written, the disciples knew Jesus had demonstrated his friendship in the profoundest way possible: he had given his life upon a cross for them.

The deepest friendships are based on self-sacrifice. Not many of us will be in situations where we're called upon to give the ultimate gift, but this doesn't mean authentic friendship is only for soldiers in bunkers or those with quickness of mind and body to throw someone out of the path of an onrushing train. Opportunities for self-sacrifice often come in smaller doses.

● *The sacrifice of encouragement.* Helping another person maximize his or her gifts can be costly. As you encourage her to be all that she can be, you may be ensuring a place for yourself on the second team. As you encourage him to scale the heights, you may eventually find yourself at a lower level of recognition.

Perhaps watching a friend succeed should be easy — even joyous — but it can be difficult. The green-eyed monster often rears its ugly head with those closest to us. It's one thing to watch the achievements of someone you don't know; it's another to have a best friend receive a call to a prestigious pulpit or have a book on the bestseller list or get elected to high office in the denomination.

But good friends learn to delight in others' gifts. When my first book was published, Woody pushed it in his congregation and invited me to preach on its theme. When he was asked to join a seminary board of trustees, I encouraged him to do it and was proud that others recognized his leadership skills.

● *The sacrifice of mercy.* A relationship between two different individuals — even the best of friends — will inevitably suffer tensions and disagreements, perhaps outright anger. We can rub each other the wrong way; we can hurt each other. No friendship will survive long without the gift of mercy.

We grant mercy when we're willing to endure the other person. Speaking of his relationship with Jack Benny, George Burns said, "Jack and I had a wonderful friendship for nearly fifty-five years. Jack never walked out on me when I sang a song, and I never walked out on him when he played the violin." We need to plan on listening to our friends' gravelly voices and screeching violins.

We also grant mercy when we forgive. A friend once reminded Clara Barton, founder of the American Red Cross, of an especially cruel thing that had been done to her years before. Miss Barton seemed not to recall it.

"Don't you remember it?" her friend asked.

"No," Barton replied, "I distinctly remember forgetting it."

Occasionally a relationship gets beat up and stomped in the dirt by something far worse than irritations; it can fall victim to brutal betrayals. By forgiveness we commit ourselves to keeping the friendship alive regardless of the wounds it has suffered.

• *The sacrifice of time.* Most of us would do almost anything short of selling our children into slavery for a little more time. There never seem to be enough minutes in the day to get through the to-do list in our Daytimers, never enough to do all God wants us to do.

Finding the time required to maintain a friendship isn't easy. But when a friend calls, you make time for a conversation, even though Mrs. Anderson has just been in to say that "many members" are concerned about the lack of pastoral visitation and you have a funeral in two hours and you have no idea about what you're preaching on Sunday even though it's already Friday. You talk and listen, and in a small way, you're laying down your life for your friend.

Being present for one another is the fundamental requirement of love, and it begins with listening. Lewis Smedes, professor at Fuller Seminary, has written, "Listening is the silent shape of caring. We listen to what the other person says to us. But we listen closest when no words are spoken. We listen for the unuttered message of feeling. We listen for pain expressed in disguised sighs. We listen for desires heard only in the language of the eyes. We listen to our own messages to learn how they were heard through the filter of the other person's needs." This kind of listening takes time.

Sometimes friendship will demand a significant sacrifice of time, far more than an hour telephone conversation.

When Kay Lewis called from Austin to tell me her husband was not doing well, I knew what had to be done. Alan and I first met in Scotland; he was my Ph.D. supervisor at the University of Edinburgh. But what began as a formal academic relationship soon developed into a deep friendship. Through the years we nurtured the relationship; hundreds of miles separated us, but visits and telephone calls kept the dialogue going on theology and politics and other good subjects.

Our recent conversations, though, had often been about cancer, his cancer. Kay called to tell me he probably would not live through the weekend. I knew I had to see him one more time. On Sunday my congregation was simply told, "Don needed to be with his friend."

From the airport I went straight to the hospital. Years of pastoral experience were not much help; professional objectivity vanishes when it's your dear friend lying there, when his wispy hair witnesses to the ravages of chemotherapy, when tubes desecrate his body, when he has barely enough strength to acknowledge your presence. It's not easy. But there's no place you would rather be.

The next day he rallied some, and the day after that brought a remarkable turnaround. At least we could talk. He reminded me of Christ's victory, the hope of the resurrection. When I needed to say goodbye — for all I knew, for the rest of this life — I knelt by his bed to pray, and then I took him in my arms, and I wept.

Alan, thank God, has not died. We continue to hope that by the grace of God he will be with us, teaching and preaching and loving, for many more years. But whatever happens, I will be present for him to the best of my ability.

C. S. Lewis pointed out that friendship is the least natural of loves: "Without *eros* none of us would have been begotten and without Affection none of us would have been reared, but we can live and breed without Friendship. The species, biologically considered, has no need of it."

Its very lack of necessity, though, underscores its relationship with grace. Friendship is a free gift, a witness to the goodness of God. One can live without friendship, just as one can live without laughter and music and books, but life would be much the poorer.

I have come to treat special friendships as something of sacramental value. Just as we believe that an extraordinary event happens when people put bread and wine together in the name of Christ, so there is an unusual occurrence when two or more commit to each another in a friendship built about Christ's name.

— *Gordon MacDonald*

CHAPTER FOUR

How to Draw Strength from People

Gail, my wife, was once cornered by a woman after an unhappy church business meeting. It had been one of our first exposures to a small Baptist congregation where some loved to battle about budgets, paint color, and the succession of church officers.

"Gail, what do you think of us all after this evening?"

"I'm really disappointed by the hurt I saw tonight," she replied.

"Oh, don't let this bother you. Gail, if you and Gordon stay here long enough, you'll learn to be just like us."

"No," my wife said. "I love you all, but I never plan to be like that."

When those words were spoken, we were barely past our mid-twenties. In that rural fellowship we were the youngest adults. Now, years later in a city church, we are the oldest people in the congregation. Then we were like a son and daughter to the people — sometimes I thought they were amused by us. Now we are like a mother and father. And sometimes I think we still amuse our congregation.

Although we've gotten older, the challenge of how to relate to a congregation has not. We continue to be concerned about creating community with members of our church. We know that without community we cannot grow into healthy spirituality; without community we cannot hope to hear the fullness of God's voice; without community we cannot hope to make a difference in the world.

So, from the Kansas prairie to the streets of New York City, I've been asking myself, *How do I cultivate community? How can I be a vital part of it and yet not be absorbed by it? How do I commit myself to it knowing that some day I'll leave? And how do I give a community leadership while submitting to it in servanthood?*

Rebuilding the Foundation

My faith tradition hasn't done adequate homework on the theological meaning of community, this despite all the recent emphasis on small groups. We understand the community demographically; we understand it therapeutically; we understand it institutionally. We use marketing techniques, psychological models, and management structures to make our communities work. But we've not yet developed a theology that convinces us that community is something more than just creating successful organizations and careers.

Let me suggest that a theology of community begins with the statement of Jesus: "Where two or three are gathered in my name, there am I in the midst." That's sacramental language. It says that something special, actually mysterious, happens when people commit to a relationship that identifies with and submits to Christ's name.

The statement exalts the group.

I am no longer satisfied hearing about having a personal relationship with Jesus Christ. This wonderful message needs balance, namely that a personal relationship with Christ means also a personal relationship to Christ's people. You accept Christ; you accept his people. The newly converted John Wesley was reminded that Christianity is not a solitary religion.

The neglect of community has resulted in an overemphasis on the leadership of solo performers: strong preachers, institutional leaders, and musicians who are viewed as oracles through whom God speaks. Preaching and organizational entrepreneurship seem synonymous with godliness.

The larger truth is that the Bible is also a book about groups, teams, communities. We must remember that God has carried on the kingdom with clusters, with groups: Moses had his Jethro, David his Jonathan, Jeremiah his Baruch, Paul his Barnabas and Silas. Even Jesus had his twelve, and especially Peter, James, and John. Assumed in the pages of Scripture is a check and balance, a consortium of gifts, a corporate witness, a sense of "We're doing this together."

Knowing the Church Community

Before pastors can decide how to relate to their churches, they need to know the make-up of those churches.

When I read between the lines of the Gospels, I see Jesus constantly making decisions about how he was going to interact with others. Some wanted his time, but he made it clear they weren't going to get it. Others felt unworthy to get anything from him, and yet, more than once, it was their homes that he visited. Jesus understood people, especially when and how he should connect with them. We're not always so sure. And we don't have many models to be sure.

Some time ago I began to realize that the people in my community tend to follow certain relationship patterns, and I described those patterns in *Renewing Your Spiritual Passion*. Although some have been disturbed by my "boxing people in," I and others have found the categories helpful. While I don't normally go around labeling people, I am helped by knowing what I can expect from various members of my community.

Very Resourceful People

VRP's are our mentors. And every time they enter our lives they bring a word of affirmation (or rebuke). They affirm our growth and effectiveness. And if we don't have a couple of these, we're missing something.

When I was a boy, my father was an extremely busy man as a church leader. I admired him and wish I'd known him better, but it wasn't possible. As a compensation God seems to have given me a string of men who have treated me as a significant human being.

No one ever impacted my life more as a VRP than Vernon Grounds, the president emeritus of Denver Seminary, where I attended. He seemed to have all the personality and spiritual traits I, as a young man, wanted most to acquire. I set out to follow him and to absorb as much of his character and view of life as I could. Hardly a day goes by now that I don't see some dimension of Vernon Grounds' personality in me, like the way he strikes up conversations with strangers. He will walk up to someone and say, "I've been looking at the smile on your face, and it's obvious to me that you're an extremely happy person." Vernon gives positive energy to everyone he engages. I always wanted to be like that, and to the extent that I am like that today, I learned it from him.

In a department store recently, I caught myself saying to a clerk, "You look to me like the vice-president for men's shirts."

That's a vintage Vernon comment: a gesture of affection that lifts the spirit of a minimum-wage clerk who feels insignificant most of the time. It elevates the conversation so that the other person feels like a peer and a friend. It offers light humor and a sense that this is more than a conversation about shirts.

Other VRP's in my older years included a Presbyterian pastor, a godly track coach, a Christian counselor, and through biographies and writings, a historical figure from the nineteenth-century Church of England, Charles Simeon.

Unlike friendships, VRP relationships usually end. Daniel Levinson's book, *Seasons of a Man's Life*, suggests that VRP relationships conclude with something called BOOM: Becoming One's Own Man. BOOM happens when the VRP releases the Very Trainable Person (VTP, which is what I was to Vernon Grounds) to his own pathway. It can be a painful process.

Usually it is the VTP who terminates the relationship because he or she becomes sure that they can make it on their own. This can be traumatic for the VRP. I have experienced that ache a few times in relationship to VTP's of my own.

But it can work the other way. The VRP has to get on with mentoring others. I remember having to adjust to the fact that Vernon Grounds had other VTP's in his life; he couldn't always be available for me. In fact, I suspect that several hundred men and women in this world each thought they were as close to Grounds as I did. This man has "fathered" a lot of spiritual children, and he hasn't stopped, although he is headed north of age 75.

The disciples were going through this to some extent when Jesus told them that he was going away. They saw nothing "expedient" (as he put it) about such a BOOM experience. And they had no concept of what he meant when he said, "Now you are my friends." They were still locked into being servants who did not know what the master was doing.

Some of my own VRP relationships have turned into friendships. Others drifted into mere pleasant memories, and I thankfully carry those memories through my life.

Very Important People

Among the VIP's in my life are my wife, Gail, my closest personal friends, people with whom I share a common call to ministry, and a broader circle of significant people who may or may not share my view of faith.

Among these people is Seth, a Jewish professor of law, who lives in our New York City apartment building. He and I frequently walk together to the Roosevelt Island tramway.

We'll banter back and forth about the latest lawyers' joke,

recent Supreme Court decisions, legal ethics, and the use of logic in argument.

Seth stretches me because he's a thinker. I feel as if I was never taught to be a thinker, that I'm always playing catch-up ball. Friends like Seth enjoy helping me do it.

Incidentally, it helps that Seth does not share my view of God or of faith. He accepts no empty words, no phrases I've used for so long that I've forgotten their real meaning. And he's not worried about saying something that would offend a preacher's ears.

My agenda with Seth is simple: I like him, and I learn by tapping his mind. I just ask questions when I'm with him. One day he gave me what I consider a high compliment, coming as it did from him: "Gordon, you ask great questions."

I enjoy having relationships with people who are quite different than me. I grew up in a system that suggested one spend time only with those who were candidates for conversion. The problem with this hit me with force one day years ago when I was conversing with my neighbor while we stood watering our lawns. I was thinking how nice it would be to know him better. But then my childhood mechanisms kicked in. I actually found myself thinking, *I'd sure like to get closer to this guy, but he's a life-long Lutheran, and there's no way he'd ever come to my church. So there's no point in pursuing this relationship.*

I came to realize I had been groomed inadvertently to evaluate people's worth on the basis of their potential to fit my agenda. From that day forward I've worked at developing relationships for nothing more than the joy of natural friendship and seeing myself as part of the broader human community. If things naturally move beyond that to issues of faith and conviction, terrific! And that has in fact happened.

My change in thinking was one reason I struck up a friendship with Mohammed, an Iraqi from Baghdad who managed a cafe in New York City. From time to time we would sip coffee together comparing our worlds: his Islamic world and my Christian one. The day the bombs started dropping in Baghdad, I stopped by the cafe and waited for him to finish his shift.

"This has got to be an awful day for you," I said. "Your family is over there, the bombs are falling, and you probably can't tell anyone around here what you're going through and expect them to understand."

"You're right," he said. "I can't tell anyone that I'm from Baghdad. So I say I'm Swedish." I made a comment about his dark eyes and his Middle Eastern complexion, and we laughed.

"Well, I know where you're from," I said. "And I want you to know that you're my friend, and I'll be praying for your family today. Let me know the first minute you hear word from them."

Mohammed wept.

On days like this, I thought, *it's not hard to have a ministry when I don't have to be anything but a cool source of water.* I've learned the joy of simplicity in relationships with people from all walks of life, and I've discovered opportunities for ministry as a serendipity.

And then there are good friends, fellow learners and "growers." I have accumulated a personal wealth in friends across North America, with whom I intersect regularly on the phone or by fax: we share book titles, interesting articles, and insightful experiences. In this cadre are three or four special friends whose worth to me cannot be estimated.

Friendship became a high priority at midlife, when I realized career achievements were worthless in contrast to being part of a network of friends who challenge each other to grow to become more useful to the kingdom.

Contemporary Christian ministry can contain a cruel payoff if one is not careful. One day I found myself asking, "Now that I've spent the better part of three decades moving around the country at the invitation of congregations and in response to what I perceived to be the call of God, who will be there for me when I am dying?"

I realized that most of a pastor's friendships are dovetailed into his or her role. Change the role and most of those friendships terminate. So who will be there, and where will they be, when you are no longer a pastor and you have another decade or two to be an old person? Who will share your aging years? Who will sit with you when you suffer loss? Who will carry your casket? Who will comfort your spouse?

Especially important to me are people I'd call "playmates" or "soulmates." These are the people with whom I enter the presence of God through prayer and mutual accountability. We keep tabs on each other's personal concerns so that we can pray for each other. We challenge each other in the development of our spirits.

I think of a recent encounter with a VIP friend. One day I went to Philadelphia to see him. Together we toured some exciting examples of city ministry. Then we went to a restaurant and sat for four hours, talking and eating Indian food. Then we polished the day off by visiting the Picasso exhibit at the Philadelphia Art Museum.

There wasn't a dead moment in the entire day. The two of us made some plans about things we want to do together in the future; we talked through endless lists of books; we discussed our frustrations with certain aspects of our faith tradition. We talked about how to stimulate one another to deeper growth. As I went home on Amtrak that evening, I typed page after page into my laptop computer — things I'd learned during the day. A time like that can keep me going for weeks.

A similar encounter happened in New York with another soulmate whom I'll call my Montreal friend. Then there are our Boston friends, a couple we've known for years and meet every month for dinner. One businessman friend occasionally checks out of his office and travels with me to a speaking engagement. I think of a friend in television; one in the world of engineering, and one in consulting. We fly in and out of each other's lives. Letters, cards, faxes, phone calls, and occasional visits with such people energize my soul.

I once said to my Philadelphia friend that there ought to be a place in friendships for one to challenge the other regularly with the question, "What's God been saying to you today?" I suggested that if that sort of accountability existed in friendship, it would bring daily meditations alive. I'd be listening hard for God's voice because I'd know someone would be checking up on me, as when Eli checked up on Samuel.

Two days later the phone rang. It was my man in Philadelphia. He didn't greet me with, "Hi, Gordon. How are you?" He just said, "What's God saying to you today?" Since that call we have a playful but serious tradition going: you get to ask the question first if you've paid for the call.

There was a time in my life when I nursed two irresponsible thoughts: I saw Gail as my best friend, and I concluded that my life was too busy for close friendships.

I don't think I'm merely fooling with words when I say that a spouse and a best friend are likely to be two different people. I am not for a moment denigrating my intimacy with Gail. I enjoy our relationship as husband and wife, and she is a wonderful friend. But I like her to be my *wife*.

I want a "best friend" to challenge me about such things as the quality of my marriage, the state of my soul, the quality of my speech, the style of my financial life, and the depth of my relationships. I don't think a spouse is in a position to do all that.

So I've relieved Gail of some of that responsibility and placed her back where I can really enjoy our relationship as husband and wife. And I've tried hard to develop several close personal friendships. That's not been easy, because my friends are incredibly busy — traveling, making decisions, running institutions, and attending conferences. We've had to learn to plan far ahead for prime times when we can look into each other's eyes and see what's going on behind them.

In terms of my relationship with Gail, we've learned to share a daily prayer discipline for our children, our friends, and for the ministry activities of our congregation. Without realizing it, we have developed all sorts of private traditions. Almost every morning we watch the same news broadcast. We eat the same foods at certain points of the week. We have a couple of favorite television shows. We take walks in the city almost every day that weather permits. During the day we exchange two or three phone calls to check on how each other is doing.

It's hard to believe that any two people can get as close as we are — especially in the past five or six years. We both know that our thirty-one years of marriage is a life investment. We don't have to keep saying it, but we are aware that our relationship was dramatically and tragically tested a few years ago. For a short while we felt as if we stood alone in our world, and during that time we entered far more deeply into each other's souls than most husbands and wives seem to do. Ever since it's been soul knitted to soul.

Other Vip's

When Gail and I came to New York, we found it easy to greatly enlarge the perimeter of our friendships. We came to understand that a lot of wonderful people are prepared to accept us just as we are. They don't treat us as a clergyman and wife, and they don't care whether or not we went to graduate school. The only credential for friendship here is that you delight in one another as human beings.

I grimace every time I hear someone speak about the hostility of New Yorkers. I find just the opposite. Gail and I have made more friends in New York than any place we've lived. When we leave the Big Apple, we will grieve over the loss of daily encounters with bus drivers, shop keepers, and doormen, mostly people of color.

One of the bus drivers used to be a sullen man. One day I told Gail I was going to get into his life one way or another. So every night when I stepped on his bus, I'd greet him with "Hello, Mr. Jessup," or "Hi, Michael" (I've changed his real name here). He rarely reacted.

One night as we neared the end of the line, the bus was virtually empty. I slipped forward and said to him, "I don't want to be nosy, but I've been looking at your face for the last few minutes, and you seem under great stress. I'm wondering if everything is all right? Is my perception a good one or bad?"

"Good perception," he grunted.

"Well, I don't know what kind of pain you're carrying, but I want you to know that when I have friends, I pray for them. So tonight when I'm getting ready for bed, I'm going to pray for you."

"Really?" he replied with surprise. "Thanks very much."

From that moment we connected. He quickly thawed, and our friendship warmed. Then one night he was blindsided in an auto accident on his way home from work. I convinced one of the other drivers to give me his unlisted number and called him.

"This is your friend, Gordon, from the island," I said when he picked up the phone. "I hear you've got migraines from the accident. I used to have them, so I know what you're going through."

"I can't believe you're calling me," he exclaimed.

"This is what friends do," I answered.

Our friendship — just one of several I have — has blossomed from that moment into the flower of banter and laughter. Recently when an embassy here in New York was bombed, he and I were talking about the pain human beings inflict upon one another.

"Do you ever get the feeling that human beings are like onions?" I philosophized. "You keep peeling back the skin and you find a different person at every level."

"Boy, is that the truth!" he affirmed.

"Of course, there are two solid exceptions to this," I quipped. "You and me." We laughed, and I exited the bus. This is what I call an uncluttered friendship, and it lifts my spirits.

Another one of my friends is someone I'll call Thomas. Last year he was mugged and left unconscious on a street corner. When he regained consciousness, he staggered to his car and, although he has no recollection of doing it, drove home.

When Thomas had been gone for some time, I spoke to some friends we have in common, "I haven't seen Thomas in a while; is he okay?"

"Thomas got beat up," someone said. "We're not even sure he's coming back. One thing's for sure; he doesn't want to talk to anyone about what happened."

Then a week later I bumped into him. "Thomas," I said, "I'm looking into your eyes, and I don't like what I see. You're in pain, aren't you?"

"Yeah."

"Have you talked to anyone about what happened?"

"No."

"Okay. Look, I'm a friend. I want to know what's happened."

We sat down, and he recounted his story. It was a horror story to be sure. I suggested that we have breakfast at my apartment the next morning, when we could have more time together.

Gail fixed a good breakfast the next day, and then she left us alone so that he could talk further without feeling humiliated. I made him retell the incident several times just so he could flush it all from his system.

When he got through and had wept a bit, I said, "I don't know how this is going to hit you, but as one brother to another, I'd like to pray for you. And when I pray for my friends, I often put a hand upon them. I'd like to ask God to expel all this terror and hurt from you."

Thomas said that would be fine, and I did as I told him I would. It was a bonding moment. In the following days, I saw his smile returning. The moment came when I was able to say, "I'm looking into your eyes, Thomas, and I see the smile coming back. I just want to see more."

Three months later Thomas invited Gail and me to his home for a family dinner. It was more than a dinner; it was a reunion. Fifty or more people were there. Thomas is from a Caribbean country; his family is East Indian. We were the only whites there. After a tremendous dinner of Indian food, Thomas stood and spoke to his family: "I want you to meet the man and woman who brought me back from the dead. Mr. Gordon, would you say some words to my family?"

I told the group about our friendship and how I continued to pray for my friend. This man is important to me. He's the sort of friend you find in the city if you're looking.

Very Trainable People

A few years ago I became convinced that men and women over 40 ought to take seriously the priority of "giving back." And giving back means pouring oneself into the younger generation. Among the younger generation are the vtp's: people who are teachable, anxious to grow, ready to follow.

The most important VTP's in my life for years were our children, Mark and Kristy. They remain the most important. But they've left home now and are married. When they come home, Gail and I do our best to be whatever they need us to be: friend or parent.

But I've not stopped parenting. In fact, I feel as if I do more of it now than ever. Years ago I was marked by a question from Carl George: Do you want to be a builder of an institution or a builder of people? I chose the latter and have no regrets.

Two of my most recent VTP's have master's degrees in business from Ivy League schools. One of the two entered my world because he was dating a young woman in our congregation. She called me one day and admitted that she was falling in love.

"Would you check him out?" she asked.

A strange question, I thought. But since he'd come to church with her a few Sundays, I had a perfect excuse to call his office and ask if we could meet for lunch. We met at midtown and ate at one of my favorite lunch spots. I liked him instantly.

We talked about his work, how he'd come to know the young woman he was dating, what he thought of her faith ("She's really into that stuff," he said), and how worship at our church had impressed him.

"I've never been any place before where people seemed so alive in their religion. I don't know what to make of it, but I'd like to become more a part of it."

"I've got a proposition for you," I said. "You come and hear me preach for a few weeks. Then let's get together for lunch again and talk about what you've heard and what you're thinking." He agreed. I went on to suggest that all of us who come near to Jesus are either spectators, seekers, followers, or kingdom builders.

After I'd described each category, he said, "I think I'm a seeker." I agreed.

Six weeks later we met again. He said, "I don't know how to describe this, but the other day I prayed and told Jesus I wanted to become a Christ-follower.''

Not many weeks later he married the woman. I introduced them to another newly married couple where the husband was also a new Christ-follower. The two couples hit it off instantly.

Then the two husbands came to me and said, ''We're married to two kingdom builders, and we're just followers. We've got to catch up. What can you do to help us?'' That's how I latched on to two new VTP's.

We've met for breakfast; this next month we have two full days scheduled together. I'm going to walk them through the Bible and show them how it's laid out. We're going to review some basic spiritual disciplines and figure out a schedule for a twelve-week covenant group in the fall. I suggested that we add four or five other men to the group and that they facilitate things so I could be the mentor and nothing else. They agreed, and so we're on.

Very Nice People

VNP's are usually swell folk. They attend church regularly; they fill the seats, sing the songs, give some of the money, and are kind to preachers. We build large and comfortable buildings and pave convenient parking lots for VNP's. (Well, in other places than New York City we build parking lots.)

Frankly I'm not sure we'd need to do that if we didn't have VNP's. The VIP's and the VTP's would come any place at any time, because they're on growth tracks, and they know what the agenda is. VNP's are not sure.

Generally the VNP's are takers more than givers. And you give them all your love and a lot of your attention, as did Jesus at times. They are the most immediate pool of people from which VTP's and VIP's may come. You pray for them; you serve them; you try to be responsive to their needs because you believe — and rightly so — that out of the crowd will come those who hear a word from God and decide that it's time to get serious about faith.

I've observed the 80/20 rule here: 20 percent of the people (VIP's and VTP's) carry the momentum and 80 percent of the people (mostly VNP's) do nothing. Under such conditions, a pastoral life begins to head toward exhaustion if the 80 percent consume your time.

You'll not find many, if any, VNP's in an Alcoholics Anonymous group. In an AA group people carry their own weight. In AA, everybody's an alcoholic, and everyone else knows it; everyone's a potential leader. But in the church people can go on indefinitely never admitting to anything, and never doing anything but coming, having fun, drawing upon resources — taking and not giving.

Nevertheless, they're a part of the community and deserve some of our attention. Jesus rarely worried about the VNP's. When they gathered in too large a number, he simply increased the volume of his call for repentance and righteousness, and that usually readjusted the size of the community.

People Most Likely to Cost You "Virtue"

Some are uncomfortable when I talk about the needy people of our congregations. But I feel a Christian leader is unwise if he or she doesn't face up to this fact: in every ministry there is a group of people who are one big bundle of struggle. Every time you encounter them, you know that "virtue is going to go out of you."

Over the years, I've realized that needy people come in different sizes and shapes.

● *Very Broken People.* Life has served up some tremendous jolts for these people: loss of job, health, or key relationships. Stress, failure, sin, betrayal, and a host of other unexpected events have simply broken their bodies or their hearts. Unfortunately, a significant number of friends disappear and become invisible when one is broken. Having no simple answers that solve the problem, they find it easy just to drop out of touch. And if someone has failed, crossed the line into sin, one's community can disintegrate.

You come into ministry expecting to spend lots of time with the VBP's. You're trained to listen to them, offer resources such as pastoral counsel and advice, refer them to other sources of aid, and pray with them.

The good thing about genuine brokenness and being a VBP is that one starts listening carefully. He or she becomes hungry for what scraps of meaning you can bring to their struggle; they are anxious to hear words of hope and grace; they suck up any prayers you have to offer. And they are usually prepared to act on what is suggested.

An authentic broken person does not stay broken for long. By the grace of God, he or she heals, and when that happens, sometimes there is a resulting strength and vitality that makes the brokenness seem worthwhile. Broken people often become one's most signal vTP's and vIP's.

I've seen brokenness, and I've known it personally. And I've learned that there is incredible power in repentance and restoration. This is a great relational "neighborhood" for a pastor to be in — among the broken people. They let you know quickly that you're important to them.

In my community I have several vBP's. I had lunch with one the other day. I found myself in touch with almost every word as he described the inner pain and humiliation he feels as a result of his failure.

When he finished talking, I said, "I could have filled in the blanks of almost every sentence you've spoken. Now let me fill in the rest of the story that you haven't even heard yet. Let's talk about what God is saying to you and what he's likely to say through you in a couple of years when this is behind you."

And you watch the healing process work. It's magnificent!

● *Very Vocal People.* One is tempted to say that the "vocals" are all words. The vvP's are those who like to get attention by talking — complaining, whining, accusing; arguing, challenging, and protesting. They're often good with words and have a facility for holding the pastor hostage to their threat of anger or criticism. One tiptoes around them in the earliest years of ministry, and that's not good. In later years one is tempted to ignore the vocals. And that's not good either.

I've tried to understand the kernel of truth the vvP is expressing. Most of the time it works.

James had a word for vvP's when he wrote: "My dear brothers, take note of this: everyone should be quick to listen, slow to speak and slow to become angry, for man's anger does not bring about the righteous life that God desires." Again he wrote, "What good is it, my brothers, if a man claims to have faith but has not deeds? Can such a faith save him?" Notice that in both places he addresses these vocals as brothers.

The monastics tell about a Russian monk who lived in a French monastery. He seemed to be a vvp, and he drove everyone crazy with his abrasive disposition and unruly mouth. The brothers used to fantasize about a monastery without him. One day they got their wish when the Russian left for Paris. But before long, the abbot of the monastery went to Paris, found the vvp monk, and brought him back. His was a simple explanation: without the Russian there was no impetus for the community to pray for grace and greater charity.

I remember that story each time I encounter a vvp in my community.

• *Very Draining People.* These are the men and women of all ages who have learned that attention can be gained by presenting people with problems. Every congregation has them.

"Drainers" often come out of homes where having problems was the only way to gain the recognition of key people. This habit is transferred to adulthood. C. S. Lewis once said something about the church being the only place that would accept these people because they've worn out their welcome in most other institutions in the world.

I confess that, when I'm tired and under pressure, I usually find creative ways to avoid the vDP's. And that's why I'll never forget a revealing moment a few years ago when one vDP confronted me and made me face the fact that I was being unpastoral.

I was standing in our church lobby talking to one of my associates when she entered from the other side. Seeing her I called out, "Hello, Millie (not her real name), how are you?" Then without pause, I turned back to conversation with my colleague.

A few seconds later I became aware that Millie was shuffling across the lobby toward us. And when she got to where we were, she stopped and faced me. In a somewhat medicated state, she spoke haltingly. I suspect that the medication broke down her inhibitions, and she said to me what others might like to have said but lacked the nerve: "Pastor Mac, you say, 'Hello, Millie, how are you?' But you really don't want to know. You turn back to your conversation and never wait for my answer."

She was absolutely correct. And I had no recourse but to apologize and admit to a dangerous busyness for which there was no excuse. I've not forgotten that moment, but that does not mean that the drainers do not test my spirit.

The drainers need the attention of people they deem to be important, whose attention can give them some sense of value. So they insist on a conversation with the pastor during every church event. They may make frequent phone calls to the office or home of the pastor. Just to know that you've concentrated on them and their perceived need is extremely important.

"I have a thought for you," I had to say to one VDP recently. "Have you noticed that you seem to need to talk to me at the end of every sermon? This is a period of time when Gail and I need to talk to newcomers and answer their questions. And yet you seem to feel that you have to talk to both of us in spite of my saying that this is time for us to spend with visitors. Do you think you could tell me why?"

It's not easy for me to confront people. But on a few occasions I've had to invite to my office those whom I believe fall into the VDP category. And I point out the behavior. Usually I offer to have an occasional conversation, and I point out that I'm not rejecting them as a friend: "But can you imagine what I'd have to do if everyone in our church wanted to have as much time with Gail and me as you ask for?"

This technique for handling the drainers has worked for me. Then again, there are times when nothing has worked, except loving bluntness.

Two Cautions

There are at least two dangers in classifying people as I've been doing here.

One is succumbing to the temptation to think people are valuable only if they're healthy and productive. But productive to whom? *Productive* is a word defined by our environment and our expectations of one another. The hurting people of the pastor's community can never be trivialized and categorized so that one's conscience can be relieved. What I've learned is that I must see people in a balanced fashion: understanding, on the one hand, the agenda people are bringing to relationships, and yet, on the other hand, seeing the possibility every person has when touched by the power of God.

One also has to be aware of a second danger: boxing people into a category. I'm thinking of a woman who is a recovering alcoholic. Some years ago she was the classic VDP by my definition. She sapped tremendous amounts of energy from Gail and me (I think Gail gets the credit for sticking it out with her). But every ounce of energy was worth it. She came to herself in an unpredictable moment and went on to enter a recovery program. Today she is a responsible woman, a VIP in her world, a source of light and strength to scores of people in recovery.

Where to Begin

In spite of the dangers, I find great value in classifying people, for reasons I've explained above. But what does one do with this analysis?

One thing is to take a look at how you spend your time. I encourage Christian leaders periodically to take their schedules and evaluate every interview they have had during the previous eight weeks. Using the several classifications, they are to assess the kind of people with whom they spend their time.

What many discover is that heavy amounts of what I call "people time" — if not the majority of people time — is spent with the VNP's, the VBP's, the VVP's, and the VDP's. What is usually troublesome is the discovery that almost no significant time is spent with the VRP's (most of us have none), the VIP's (most of us have few, and those we have, we tend to engage only when convenient), and the VTP's (most of us have not sought them out).

I call these latter people "my personal connection." These are the people who bring powerful refreshment to my mind and soul. I call the others "my primary circle of possibilities." And I've learned to put those in my personal connection on the calendar first. Then I permit those in my circle of possibilities to fit in afterwards.

That approach turns some people off. They suggest that Jesus would be horrified by such a notion. But the fact is he did exactly as I am doing. Those I'd number among his "possibilities" got their time with him, but not comparable to what he gave to his VRP (the Father), his VIP's (perhaps Peter, James, and John), and his VTP's (the twelve and a few score others, including Mary, Martha, Lazarus).

When pastors have coded the people-time entries in their date books, I challenge them to build a "phantom week," a schedule based on what they think a model week should look like in terms of people time. You've got 168 hours. Where do the connection people fit in (your spouse, your children, your VRP's, VIP's, and VTP's)? Obviously they're not all going to fit into one week. But what would make a healthy week? It's an interesting game, and it's not that easy to play.

Since I'm an introvert by temperament, my circle of connections is a tighter circle than the circle Gail draws. I have to broaden my circle (sometimes I think she has to shrink hers). In the past few years, I've worked hard at it. I came to see that it was a serious flaw in my life. As I've gotten older, I've diminished VRP time, enlarged VIP time, and tried to greatly enlarge VTP time. And, frankly, I've found some time by squeezing it from the VNP's, VVP's, and VDP's. The VBP's, genuinely broken people, I'll always try to be available for.

No one can pretend that they are mastering personal growth if they've not spent time in an inventory of their relationships. In every one of the categories there's been something to give and something to receive. And growth is the bottom line of it all.

Part Three
The Renaissance
Reverend

From the earliest pages of Scripture, the growing person is challenged to monitor the soul, for feelings, attitudes, motives, prevailing spiritual conditions. The failure to do so regularly is an invitation to a shrinking spirituality.

— Gordon MacDonald

CHAPTER FIVE

Working with Your Emotional Type

Some years ago I visited with a faculty member of the prep school I attended as a teenager. At the time my son, Mark, was 13 years old, and so I wasn't surprised when asked if he would be following in my footsteps and enrolling in the school. Sending Mark there would have meant a geographical separation of three states and seeing him only on vacations.

"No, he won't be coming," I responded, startling even myself with the hastiness of my answer.

"Can I ask why?" the question came back.

I heard myself say, "Frankly, I love Mark and enjoy him so much that I'm not prepared to part with him. He not only needs me as his father, but I need him. He is my only son."

When I said those words, I suddenly felt a powerful streak of rage sweep through my entire body. It began at my toes and moved to the top of my head. I actually began to shake.

It took me several days to understand what had happened. For the first time I discovered a cluster of feelings that had been seething deep in my soul for twenty-five years. They were based on an impression (of doubtful accuracy) that my parents had not felt the same way about me when they sent me away to school.

Actually, my father and mother saw a boarding school education as one of the best things they could give me. For them it was an act of love. But I could no longer deny that, along with the great blessing I'd been given, I'd repressed the feeling that I'd been cut loose from the family, that I was no longer wanted.

It was scary to realize that this anger had been inside me that long. It made me ask, "What other feelings and misperceptions are deep within, feelings I've never processed and properly packed away? Are they inhibiting my growth, my ability to be a liberated person?"

I've read psychology books, so I know about the phenomenon of repression. But I assumed that this was the habit of unhealthy people, and I didn't see myself as unhealthy. As a pastor, I'd helped a few people deal with repressed feelings, and I had always done it with a slight air of self-confidence, assuming I never had to worry about these sorts of things.

But in the wake of this conversation about my son leaving home, I discovered a shocking fact about myself: Anger had been smoldering silently within me for twenty-plus years. Now it had exploded like a car bomb.

That experience taught me the importance of constantly monitoring the soul for those things from the past. They lie in the inner catacombs, sending up occasional strange and undecipherable signals — feelings, attitudes, desires, and motives all positioned to surprise us in temptations, resentments, and inappropriate reactions.

Some of us try rushing through life never respecting this fact of our interior lives. We weep in strange places and do not know why. We have flashes of unpredictable indignation over small things and can't explain it. We react to certain personality styles, show inordinate frustration in particular situations, struggle with certain doubts and fears. We deny, avoid, enslave ourselves — a score of differing and often unexplainable actions and patterns. And we are oblivious that much of this is being driven by the deeper and darker parts of self, parts we have never brought to light nor permitted Jesus to heal and order.

I remember watching the Secret Service and street mainte-nance people of our community weld shut the sewer lids on Massa-chusetts Avenue as they prepared for a visit by the President of the United States. They were taking no chances that a terrorist might pop out of one of those holes with a bomb. So the whole under-ground system was sealed shut.

An apt metaphor, I think, for many men and women in lead-ership. Seal the entrances to the inner world. That way nothing gets out. I don't have to go deep and face the fact that beneath my public personage is an ordinary, needy, and often desperately sinful hu-man being.

That part of our past we do not like to face. But some things about our present history we do not know well either. I believe we not only need to know what's deep within us but also our natural preferences: the instinctive ways we think, intersect with people, make decisions, and bring structure to our worlds. We all have patterns by which we operate. We grow faster and better if we have an understanding of these patterns, as well.

My father and I had a wonderful conversation not long ago. It was a great contrast to other times when we've struggled to under-stand one another, ending up feeling alone and misunderstood. This time, though, I was able to identify something significant.

My father is driven by what he believes is the truth of each situation. His passion is for logic, consistency, evidence, and cor-rectness. That's not a bad list. But it often makes my father come across as a tough, blunt, sometimes unfeeling person. He says what he thinks, and he does not change his mind easily. As a boy I had interpreted these characteristics negatively and assumed that he didn't like me and was disappointed in me.

I'm different. I'm driven by a concern for human relationships and connections. I'm concerned about how people are being affected by what's going on. Are they excited, hurt, motivated, angered? Will these words or events unify, make people feel better, help them grow?

It's not that I'm not concerned for truth. I just want to make sure that the other person can handle the truth without being unnecessarily devastated by it. So I'm always monitoring the environment of relationships, asking questions about timing, correct wording, and potential success or disaster.

That means that conversations between my dad and me are uneven — almost like a boxing match between a slugger and a puncher. We get on a topic, and he smashes away, wanting to win, wanting to persuade, wanting to make every point relentlessly and remorselessly. And I bob and weave, trying to make my points "surgically."

I don't want to offend him, be too blunt, hurt his feelings. I'm prepared to walk back to my corner having taken all of his blows, but I'm reluctant to club him to the floor. His feelings are more important to me than winning.

It wasn't until recently that I've been able to identify and put labels on this difference between us. Then we had that exchange, in which, in the middle of a discussion, I said to him, "Dad, the problem you and I have is this: When you go at truth, you're an 'engineer,' concerned only about the precision of your facts. I'm a 'poet.' I love beauty and meaning. You don't seem to consult your feelings; I may listen too much to them."

He thought about that for a moment, made a comment like, "If you say so," and then returned to his argument. But for me it was a moment of revelation that brought me greater peace with my father and made it easier to love him.

Some of those who study differences like these refer to them as "personality types." When I began to discover some things about my personality type, I was astounded. All sorts of new ways emerged for me to understand myself, my wife, and my friends. But most importantly, I discovered a lot about how I relate to Jesus as Lord and what is the likely way for me to pursue a deeper spirituality.

I'm suggesting here that personal growth is greatly enhanced when we do our homework on two areas of our lives: our past personal history (the inner tour) and our present personal history (an inventory of our personality).

Getting in Touch with the Past

The pastor or Christian leader who wants to grow has to be in touch with himself or herself — first, on this issue of what baggage we are carrying from the past. In some places I might say to a group, "There are all sorts of 'demons and dragons' (I put these words in quotes because I do not mean them in a theological sense) slithering about in the depths of our souls." Or using spy language, I might say that within us exist "moles and sleepers." They have to be caught and identified, understood and named. I'm not advocating an introspection that becomes morbid and self-preoccupying, only that we need to deal with this interior stuff, or it — the 'demons and dragons' — will deal with us.

Many are the persons in leadership who cannot handle criticism or disagreement. They have to win, always be right, or have the best idea. Some are given to angry outbursts, irrational defensiveness, brief periods of melancholy, unexplained feelings of bitterness against rivals. These are all evil behaviors that can cripple the person who has never asked, "Why? What's behind these attitudes? What's down there?"

It's not enough to say, "I'm a sinner." That's not bad for a start, of course. But what has ignited these untoward behaviors? What's the fuel for these sinful fires? This may sound crazy, but I'd speculate that the more dramatic and unusual a leader's success as a personality, as a communicator, and as an organization builder, the more he or she has to explore the interior world. Sometimes unusual and passionate efforts are fueled by great personal disturbances of the past as much as they are fueled by noble motivations.

The Catholic monastics understand this. It's one of the reasons every brother in the order must submit to spiritual direction. Even the abbot of the monastery must regularly remove himself from his position of authority and submit to the searching questions of a confessor. This he does lest he weld the sewer lids tight and forget that good and noble needs do not always have good and noble motivations.

We in the Reformation tradition renounced the notion of confessing one's sins to a priest and celebrated the right to confess our sins privately to the heavenly Father. In correcting one point, we missed another: the inner journey is probably best not taken alone. We are either too soft on ourselves or too hard on ourselves. A fellow traveler can give us perspective. The monks know this.

The psalmist prays, "Search me, O God, and know my heart." He goes on to pray that wicked ways will be exposed. Jeremiah calls the heart a wicked and incomprehensible thing. They are both alluding to the problem I'm raising: within each of us is a bottomless pit of mysteries. Growth means taking the hand of Jesus and walking deep into that pit and naming what is found.

It's not enough to come to prayer confessing this specific and that. When a pattern emerges over many times of confession, it's time to ask, "Why? What's behind this persistent activity I have to bring to the cross so frequently?"

We've made the mistake of thinking that confession is merely a legal transaction between God and ourselves. I confess a sin, and God forgives it. *Great*, we conclude, *the slate is wiped clean.*

But if we deal only with the single act and show no curiosity concerning the possibility of roots beneath the act, our confession is nearly worthless. It will bring only temporary relief. The behavior will most likely return in the same form or in another. In this sort of confession, only a "branch" of behavior has been pruned, not the roots.

And if one wishes to go deeper, one will find that at the root of the "roots" one has an awful lot of evil. This irrational, destructive evil is just there, and it lies in wait to inhibit the nobility that God meant for us to express. Jeremiah was right: who can figure out the heart? I find the answer only in a relationship with Jesus and in community with the people who follow him.

Mastering personal growth means facing up to all of this, not just periodically when something wrong has happened but consistently. Repentance is a spiritual lifestyle, not an occasional event when we have done something really bad.

The good news is that a certain liberation comes when one is conscious of the inner journey:

• *Increased personal energy.* In the years when I used to drive my 36-horsepower Volkswagen across the Colorado plains, it was not unusual to hit stiff head winds coming off the mountains. More than once I had to shift down into third and even second gear to keep going against the wind.

I still made progress. But in the lower gear I moved at a slower speed, increased my use of gas, and put greater wear and tear on the engine.

This describes something of what happens when we've not done our interior homework. What earlier I called demons and dragons, moles and sleepers, can also be called head winds. And when they begin to blow furiously, we are slowed up. The result? Fatigue of the spirit.

In the last couple of years of my pastorate at Grace Chapel in Lexington, Massachusetts, I began to drive in second gear. In the earlier years of ministry, I had enjoyed a wonderful sense of "over-drive." But as the institution of the church grew, I found myself giving less attention to the things I really enjoyed doing.

My pastoral role had became that of a CEO — and I was probably not a very good one. I made administrative decisions, met with staff and lay leaders, and wrestled with questions no one else in the line of responsibility felt ready to answer. It became a tremendous emotional drain.

In the earlier years I was much freer to be with the congregation in worship, and in a more spontaneous way. Now things were structured and formatted, so much so that I couldn't use the very strengths I earlier had brought to the congregation. That I did not see this was no one's fault but my own.

As I walked to the front of the sanctuary to greet people after the third morning worship service, I'd dream about escaping through one of the side doors. I learned to avoid eye contact with people I didn't want to talk to.

I should have done an intensive self-exploration at that point. In fact, I should have found someone who would have walked me through the exercise and forced truth out of me, truth I wasn't able to face alone.

More specifically, I should have asked myself, *Why does this not seem fun anymore? Why do I look forward to speaking opportunities outside of New England more than my work right here? Why am I finding it harder and harder to convince the lay leadership of a right course of action? Why do I find myself giving in to people every time they disagree with me? Why do I want to avoid tough critics? Why am I showing anger at innocuous things and showing no reaction to things worth getting angry about?*

The truth was I was in second gear, working harder, achieving less. I was drifting toward my weaknesses and moving away from my God-given strengths.

Driving in second gear is the perfect environment for the Evil One to derail a leader. Today when I hear of a man or woman in leadership falling into personal failure, I'm slow to make the quick, harsh judgments that I hear so many Christians make. I've come to learn the hard way that behind every failure is a web of spiritual intrigue. The issue is usually not the specific failure that gains everyone's attention; the issue is the drain of spirit that happened over months and maybe years, a drain that causes a person to become weak enough so that the final sin is simply a "straw that broke the camel's back." First comes fatigue, then comes deceit, and then comes defeat.

When a person ends up making a fatal choice for failure, he or she must accept responsibility for it. But maybe we have to require more the mutual, corporate responsibility for creating a system of faith and community that requires leaders to make regular journeys into the soul, to find out what lies in ambush.

- *Better control in tense situations.* A lot of us never learned to express accurately our feelings when we were children. Growing up, I became afraid of anger because I'd seen its destructiveness in the lives of other people. Besides, my perception was that a Christian wasn't ever supposed to be angry. So I never developed a mature adversarial style.

If someone disagreed with me, I simply backed off and came at the issue in another way. As the years went by, that sort of process cost me dearly. I learned that I had to become more candid and confrontive.

I found that I had a habit of being concerned about everyone else's feelings but not my own. Wasn't that the virtuous thing? Wasn't that servanthood? Isn't the pastor a sacrificial person? That's what I thought others were thinking, that I put others before myself. But what I was doing was not virtuous. It was partly temperament, a tendency to underreact in tense situations.

Gail has been extremely helpful to me in this area. She helps me identify what exactly I'm feeling, and that helps me know how to handle tense situations. She carefully pushes me with "What is the prevailing feeling in you today?" And if I can't identify my emotions, she'll give me a multiple-choice test.

Since I didn't do a good job on this when I was young, I've been playing catch-up. At midlife, it's becoming clearer to me that lots of feelings have to be identified and dealt with. When you don't deal with them, they take on different shapes and forms and begin to control you.

I've spent some time meditating on the feelings of Jesus and his willingness to express them. Look at his range of expressed emotions: anger, sadness, humor, gloom, joy. They're all there — not repressed but vented in proper ways at appropriate levels.

• *Relief from unnecessary guilt.* The interior journey has helped me sort out real guilt from manufactured guilt. My faith tradition emphasizes holy behavior and strong commitment, but that emphasis has a tendency to create expectations to reach the never reachable. To the extent that this happens, we are candidates for manufacturing guilt for ourselves and others.

"All you ever do is tell me what I'm not doing right or not doing enough of," a plain-spoken layman once told me when I was a young, impetuous preacher. And he was right. I'd fallen for the notion that if you can make them feel guilty, you've blessed them. This layman didn't realize, though, that if I created guilt for him, I was creating much larger doses of it for myself. I was my own worse critic.

The interior journey can militate against this tendency. It can sort out the true biblical rebukes from the superficial ones.

● *Increased sensitivity.* Not long ago Gail and I had lunch with a couple in their eighties. At one point, I asked the man, "Do you two fight any more?"

"Yeah, we fight," he responded.

"How do you handle your conflicts?"

"Well, we had one this morning," he said. "Alice (not her real name) was driving, and she made a very bad decision." We all laughed.

"What did you do?"

"I learned some years ago that it's not wise to tell Alice what I'm thinking right away. So I said to her as we drove along, 'Darling, when you have a free moment, I have a thought for you.' I know that when Alice was a girl, her father was often harsh with her. Whenever she hears a correction, she's reminded of that pain with her father. So I have to be both gentle and timely."

That conversation was my first realization that people in their seventies and eighties still live with childhood hurts. But I also saw an extremely mature man who had learned how to be sensitive to that fact. If something difficult had to be said, he would make sure it was said in a moment when she was prepared and could handle it, without increasing her anxiety unduly or calling up pain from the past.

I would like to think I've always been a sensitive man. But the truth is I haven't been — not nearly enough. I've thought I've known the needs of the people in the pews. But there came a time in my life when I left the pulpit and sat in the pew. What I learned left me astonished. I realized I had hardly known the people in the pew. I had guessed their needs; I didn't really know them. And as a result, my sermons, my prayers, my simplistic comments could not effectively reach out to the pain and struggle in which most people found themselves. When I became broken before God in a humiliating moment, I learned that there is a lot of stuff inside the soul — mine and others — that I'd never explored.

I've learned to make a search of the interior a part of my spiritual discipline. Here are some routine questions to ask:

• Is there any unfinished business in the soul from yesterday that has to be addressed? Words and deeds and thoughts that could be an offense to Jesus or to the people of your community?

• What are the prevailing feelings this morning? What are you hearing your heart say?

• Are you on the defense or the offense today when it comes to kingdom building?

• Are you at peace in your primary circle of relationships?

• Do you have a respect for sin? And a hatred of it?

Being in Touch with My Present Self

This matter of temperament is a second issue. The previous question had to do mainly with the past. This issue deals with what I am right now and what I am capable of becoming.

One of the great learning experiences for Gail and me has been being introduced to the Myers-Briggs Temperament Inventory. It doesn't explain everything, but it does give me concepts that help me identify my inner makeup and understand why I react the way I do. That has helped me grow spiritually and in pastoral effectiveness.

The MBTI is one of several systems built upon serious research, and it has been useful in business, education, and the military. Many Christian organizations have used it to match people to task. And some marvelous things have been written about how personality type helps us understand our own spirituality, how we each encounter God in unique ways.

A crazy example: In the middle of a worship service, I often ask people to turn around and greet each other. Some people enjoy doing that. They like to engage everyone around them. Others cringe. I used to think these people were just plain grouches, and I'd wonder why they were so resistant to common Christian fellowship.

Now I know that a serendipitous encounter grates against their type. They can be friendly when they want, but their instinct is to prefer anonymity and space. It's not a spiritual problem for them; it's a preference due to type.

Of the many good books that discuss the Myers-Briggs way of looking at people, I like best *Please Understand Me* by David Kiernsey and Marilyn Bates. In brief, the MBTI people have identified eight personality types, falling into four contrasting pairs.

Introvert/Extrovert: How Do I Restore My Energy?

By now you've figured out that I'm an introvert, that I gather energy by being alone. I'm never afraid to be alone. One of Gail's most wonderful gifts to me was to send me off to Switzerland one year to walk the Alps by myself. For two weeks, I walked alone, not one significant conversation with anyone. I was renewed.

But introverts are not hermits. They enjoy a few intense friendships rather than many. They have an extremely large inner world. I've often felt that 90 percent of my world exists within myself.

Extroverts are just the opposite. They are energized by being with people. Give extroverts a free evening, and they'll think of a list of people they could share it with.

Gail is an extrovert. Normally, she loves to be with people, working, learning, playing with them. She thinks best in concert with others.

While I usually think before I say anything, especially in conflict, she is inclined to speak as she thinks. She calls it (I would never say this myself) "noisy thinking." If we are debating something, she says whatever she is thinking, and I have to guess at her ultimate conclusion. That can be exasperating. But even more exasperating to her is my behavior: I back off into introverted silence until I've decided upon my fixed and final position.

Gail loves to pray with people, and that's one reason why it's important to her that we pray regularly together. As an introvert, I could easily do all my praying by myself. But we've learned to compromise on this one. And I'm blessed by entering her extroverted world, and I think she's caught a little of my introversion for herself.

It's helpful to know I'm an introvert because I can now choose to act like an extrovert when I need to — for instance at the mandatory wedding reception, or church picnic, or Sunday morning social hour. When I didn't understand my recoiling at the thought of such events, I felt guilty and resented those who sought my attendance.

Now, knowing my temperament, when I feel like slipping out a side door, I can suck in my breath and say to myself, "Well, Mr. Introvert, charge into that group and get to know everyone you can. There will be plenty of time to be alone after it's over."

And it works; I know why I don't want to do it and why I should.

One gets the feeling that Jesus was able to feel comfortable as both extrovert and introvert. He was at ease when alone; he was quite at home in the midst of a group. Growth for me means being an introvert who can encounter the crowd and feel perfectly at ease.

Intuitive/Sensate: How Do I Take In Information?

Gail is a sensate. She sees her world through form, color, structure, and proportion. She's intensely aware of everything that comes to her through the five senses. When she walks into a room, she immediately responds to the way it's decorated, thinking, *Do the colors match? Are the picture frames at the right height? Is the desk orderly?* She says her stomach reacts to a mismatch of colors.

Sensates, thank the Lord, are also practical. They love details and manage them well. Orderliness is important. So are things like promptness and dependability. I married a woman who loves an organized closet, a reconciled checkbook, an up-to-date address and phone list, and a myriad of birthday cards all sent out on time. I am a fortunate man.

Now Gail — sad for her — married an intuitive who is slightly color blind and, by nature, disorganized, a man who has to write books like *Ordering Your Private World* to get his act together. We intuitives are drawn toward issues like meaning and vision. If Gail walks into a room asking what the decorator did, I walk in trying to figure out what the decorator was trying to say.

I'm into dreams, symbols, hidden meanings, possibilities, ideas. It often means that I'm a daydreamer, staring off into space, thinking about things that might never be. The downside is that I worry too much, can easily paint pessimistic pictures, or get myself so convinced of an idea that I cannot fathom whether or not it is practical. Gail helps me here.

You can tell Gail and I differ in temperament from the way we listen to a story. Someone begins to relate a tale to us, and Gail halts the narrative every once in a while to ask a clarifying question. My reaction is one of consternation: "Honey, let the man tell the whole story, and then we'll get to the questions." But Gail doesn't want to move ahead without clarifying details. I want to hear the whole story first. Then maybe we'll have time to brush over the details.

Some people might think that we intuitives are the deeper people. But what good is all our "depth" if we get nothing done? As an intuitive, I'm a starter of projects because everything interests me — to a point. I struggle to finish things. In contrast Gail's a finisher. So she never starts anything she doesn't intend to complete. Gail never has to worry about deadlines; I live in the shadow of their tyranny all the time.

All intuitives need sensates in order to keep their feet on the ground. All sensates need intuitives lest they become earthbound. Jesus was both. His intuitive side is working when he sees strong possibilities in people, when he talks about the gospel being preached to the nations. His sensate side is showing when he enjoys lilies, eating, and planning for upper room gatherings.

I'm finding a growth experience in breaking free of my intuitive habits and becoming more sensate. Thank God for computers. Their software for personal organization — reminders about cards, appointments, commitments — has become an extension of my forgetful brain. I have a way to go yet, but I'm growing.

Feeling/Thinking: How Do I Process Information?

The Myers-Briggs folks say that feelers are more sensitive to people and thinkers more concerned with issues, facts, and evidence — remember me and my father?

Gail and I are both feelers. We tend to evaluate all truth on the basis of how it's going to affect people. We instinctively ask, "What's this going to do to John? Mary? Who is hurting here? What possibilities are there for growth and development? Is someone neglected? Who needs affirmation?"

Feelers instantly sense conflict between people. Both of us walk into a room and within seconds we begin assessing the moods and attitudes of people. We read faces, body language, tones of voice, and choices of words. And we are usually drawn to those we sense are in trouble.

We have a close friend who is a thinker "off the charts," as we say. He is a person for whom the truth of the idea is all important. He says exactly what he thinks. And he sometimes seems oblivious to how it affects people around him. Sometimes when we're together, we laugh at our differences, lest we cry.

Sometimes his opinions seem harsh and non-negotiable. But it's this commitment to the truth that has made him an effective leader. Fortunately for him, his wife is a feeler, and she is able to mitigate any potential insensitivity he might display. All together, he handles himself well.

This type makes a difference in one's pastoral style. We feelers are extremely conscious of how a congregation is reacting to a program or a sermon. We worry a lot about unity, love, and people getting appreciation. Thinkers believe that people need to hear the truth — even if it hurts. They're convinced that speaking the truth is the best way to motivate people to change.

They tell us feelers that we're too subjective, too wishy-washy: "Why can't you be more like Luther and Calvin?" And we feelers say, "Why can't you be more like St. Francis and Corrie ten Boom?"

We feelers are tempted to soften the truth if we can maximize the well-being of people for the short term; thinkers assume we're compromising, and they go on and on speaking the truth, running the risk of splitting a group with their non-negotiables.

Again, Jesus was both thinker and feeler. When he was with Pharisees who kept trying to cover up the truth, Jesus was at his best as a thinker. "Face facts," he'd say to them. And then he'd speak the facts. It really didn't bother him a bit that he made men angry. Truth was truth; someone had to say it.

But Jesus was also a feeler. It was thinkers who brought the adulterous woman to Jesus. It was Jesus the feeler who saw her pitiable condition and sent her on her way with a relatively soft "Go and sin no more." Jesus the thinker delayed going to Lazarus's bedside; Jesus the feeler wept at his grave.

It would have been helpful for me had I known this language years ago. Now I understand why I was never drawn to heavy theology. By temperament I was put off by those who seemed to waste hours straining over the meaning of a word or an obscure idea. I had troubling visceral feelings when I heard people arguing to the point of schism.

Our seminaries would be helped here if they understood that a high percentage of pastoral candidates are feelers — who have high people values — who are shoved through an educational process that is managed and staffed mainly by thinkers. It's surprising that the feelers and thinkers connect as well as they do in most seminaries. But it is not surprising (although it is significant) that feelers often end up complaining that their seminary education was largely irrelevant to them.

Personal growth for me has meant understanding myself as a feeler, enjoying its strengths, and being wary of its downsides. It has meant pushing myself to become more of a thinker. I've learned not to react to the tough words of the thinker, who usually has no intention of hurting me. And I've had to learn that my feeling perspective will not always reach the thinker if I don't understand his or her temperament and language.

Perception/Judgment: How Do I Make Decisions?

What gray hairs Gail now owns come from having to cope with me in this category. For I am what the MBTI people call "a perceiver." Gail is a judger. And perceivers and judgers go about making decisions in entirely different ways.

Perceivers enjoy the process of working through decisions. We talk and think and talk and think. We conjure up all the options, consult all the sources of expertise, worry about unexpected possibilities. We like to keep all of our options open until the very last minute. In fact, we don't like "last moments." Our only problem in decision making is making the decision. We worry about making a decision because we're afraid that when we do, a new piece of data will show up that would have caused us to go in another direction. So we prefer serendipity, "going with the flow."

Gail, on the other hand, is a judger. I tell her that she never saw a decision she didn't like to make. If I struggle to come to closure on decisions, she likes to come to closure too swiftly. I love to kid her about jumping to conclusions; she loves to kid me about treating conclusions as if they were diseased.

Because Gail is a judger, she loves to structure her world and get as many decisions in hand as possible. That's why I can frustrate her when she asks what I'd like to do Friday evening. I say, "I don't know; we'll have to see what the weather is like." And then when I ask her why she needs to know on Tuesday what we're going to do on Friday, she'll answer, "I'm trying to decide what I'm going to wear."

Some studies suggest that a large percentage of pastors are perceivers. And if they are, they have to realize why they might have trouble with church board members who are judgers. Perceivers want to string out the process. They may even keep delaying decisions by saying they need more time to pray. The judgers are demanding that we get on with things: "Let's decide what we want to do and do it!"

Again, growth for me has been to face up to the strengths and weaknesses of being a perceiver. I am aware of my tendency to put off decisions, and by knowing this, I can deliberately assume a judger's stance and get decisions made that I once used to delay.

Since decision making is a difficult process for me, I've learned to welcome team decisions. I find that by becoming part of a staff team at church, more decisions are made, and more quickly, than if I mull them over myself. So I'm quick to ask for the aid of others.

It's clear that Jesus knew exactly how to manage these temperaments as they were fully expressed in his own personality. "He set his face toward Jerusalem" is the act of a judger, one who can make a decision. But the perceiver is in motion when he says to Simon Peter, "I have prayed for you that your faith may not fail. And when you have turned back, strengthen your brothers." He sees and accepts that Peter is in process.

Putting It Together

In Genesis, there is a brief, interesting dialogue between God and Cain. God takes note of something about which Cain seems oblivious: his anger toward Abel, his brother.

This ancient story is prepsychology, of course. But any psychologist would have to be comfortable with what's going on here. God is inviting Cain to an interior journey. He reads the signal of a sullen face and says, "Why are you angry? Why is your face downcast?"

He's asking Cain to look inside, to inventory his feelings and attitudes. God sees what Cain is trying to avoid: the "demons and dragons" swimming in Cain's soul. If they are not named and dragged to the surface, they will soon influence Cain's will, and he will do something terribly destructive.

But Cain cannot or will not submit to the inventory. He is in denial. And the result is tragedy, for Abel and Cain.

From the earliest pages of Scripture the growing person is challenged to monitor the soul, for feelings, attitudes, motives, prevailing spiritual conditions. The failure to do so with regularity is an invitation to a shrinking spirituality.

Sometimes in my own spiritual disciplines I think I hear God's voice saying, "Gordon, why are you down today?" or "Why that gesture of impatience when the phone rang?" or "Why are you resistant to quiet?" or "Why are you avoiding praying with Gail?" These are the Cain questions. They are asked when the issues within are simple and manageable. But avoided, the issues within grow complex and unmanageable. The "demons and the dragons" are in motion again.

Then there's the story of Paul and Barnabas debating about John Mark. Paul, the thinker, can look at John Mark and only say that the young man is a failure and unworthy of a second chance.

But Barnabas is a feeler. Facts may be important. But he's looked into the heart of John Mark. He sees growth and new possibilities. As a people person, Barnabas believes John should have a chance for a new start. Barnabas believes in the process.

The thinker and the feeler disagreed so strongly on this matter that they parted company. I could be wrong, but I think Paul did the parting. A feeler would have stayed around and kept trying to find a compromise on the issue. But that's speculation, and thinkers will disagree with me (but I'm not giving in!).

John Mark went on to be a champion. And even Paul came to admit to the profitability of the man. Too bad the thinker didn't see it soon enough.

Knowing what's in my past helps me bring things to the cross. Knowing what's presently in my temperament helps me serve Christ more effectively. Knowing both contributes a lot to my potential personal growth.

But none of this makes sense unless it's done in the company of Jesus, and as I've already hinted, also done in the fellowship of the brothers and sisters.

Study waits quietly, almost helplessly, like a doctor who can't get near a victim because of the frantic activity surrounding the scene of the accident. So when I'm wise, I clear a way for study, protecting it in every way possible.

— *Donald McCullough*

CHAPTER SIX

Enlarging the Mind to Expand the Ministry

There was a time when pastors worked in *studies;* now we work in *offices.* This reflects, at least in part, a change in perceptions about the pastoral role. Jonathan Edwards and his eighteen hours of daily study may still be mentioned in reverent tones by seminary professors seeking to inspire scholarly excellence, but today's pastor will likely find a more congenial model in Lee Iacocca.

The modern church, with its plethora of programs, seems to want administrators more than theologians. Successful pastors' conferences don't offer theological lectures; they provide training in management techniques.

So why study? It's an important question considering the contemporary expectations heaped on pastors. Why study when you could be developing strategies to attract newcomers? Why study when you could be creating flow charts for more effective congregational communication? Why study when you could be defining goals and honing objectives?

How can you justify sitting alone at your desk to work through a section of Karl Barth's *Church Dogmatics* when Mrs. Brown lies in a hospital bed, terrified of her upcoming surgery? How can you possibly luxuriate on an island of solitude when all around rages a stormy sea of human misery?

Why Study?

Simply put, we have no choice: if we've been ordained to the ministry of the Word, we must work to understand both God's Word and the world to which we proclaim it.

John Stott has developed the metaphor of bridge building: "If we are to build bridges into the real world, and seek to relate the Word of God to the major themes of life and the major issues of the day, then we have to take seriously both the biblical text and the contemporary scene. We cannot afford to remain on either side of the cultural divide . . . it is our responsibility to explore the territories on both sides of the ravine until we become thoroughly familiar with them." Only then shall we discern the connections between them and be able to speak the divine Word to the human situation with any degree of sensitivity and accuracy.

Our study of these diverse worlds doesn't simply provide a file of facts for spicing up a dull sermon. Study changes us; it provides a broad context, delivering us from the narrow dimensions of personal experience.

A popular myth holds that personal experience is the only adequate teacher. Fred Craddock points out the fallacy of this notion: "A soldier in the trenches of the Civil War came to understand war in ways unavailable to noncombatants. However, that experience was also limiting; so limiting, in fact, that the soldier could

hardly interpret that war to the nation and to subsequent genera-
tions. That task calls for another perspective, that is, another experience. Getting distance from an event and reflecting on it is experience
as surely as being plunged into its swirling currents. Study is not an
alternative to experience but is itself a form of experience that grants
understanding, even expertise, on a range of subjects."

As valuable as my own experiences are, they are too small, too
cramped for my ministry. But through Augustine's *Confessions*, I
enter into the spaciousness of one of the greatest minds of the
ancient world; through Calvin's *Institutes of the Christian Religion*, I
have my understanding of God stretched and ordered beyond my
own natural abilities; through Tolstoy's *Anna Karenina*, I discover
the ecstasy and terrible pain of adultery; through *The Autobiography
of Malcolm X*, I become a black man, and have kindled within me the
fires of anger over racism. Study lifts me to a higher and wider
plane.

Billy Graham addressed a gathering of clergy in London in
1979. He said that if he had his ministry to do over again, he would
study three times as much as he had and would take on fewer
engagements.

"I've preached too much," said Graham, "and studied too
little."

This is a regret we don't want to discover near the end of our
own ministries. We want to sink deeply the pylons of the bridge in
both the soil of God and the soil of humanity.

Finding Time

I've pastored both a small church and a large church, and I've
discovered little difference: there never seems enough time for
study. Opportunities for reading are as scarce as pine trees on
Southern California beaches. But if you know where to look, the
occasional Torrey Pine can be seen; time for study can be found.

When we pastors get together, complaints about our busy
schedules surface immediately. Clergy magazines are filled with
themes of weariness, burnout, stress. Yes, pastors are busy. But we
sometimes forget we have been given a wonderful gift — the gift of

time. When we were installed as pastors, most of us were released from the burden of having to earn an income and given great freedom (in general) to invest ourselves in the tasks we deem important.

During the French Revolution, political prisoners were incarcerated in dingy dungeons. There is a story about a state's prisoner who possessed a Bible. His cell mates were eager to hear him read, but the darkness prohibited him from seeing the words. The only shaft of light fell through a tiny window near the ceiling, and this for only a few minutes each day. The prisoners, then, would lift the owner of the Bible onto their shoulders and into the sunlight. There, in that position, he would study. Then they would bring him down and say, "Tell us now, what did you read while you were in the light?"

The church, through ordination, has lifted pastors on its shoulders and commissioned them to study on its behalf. If we fail in this task, it's not because we don't have the time; it's because we've not made good use of the time we've been given. For me, the real problem has been lack of discipline.

When I started my Ph.D. work at the University of Edinburgh, I was forced to face some uncomfortable tendencies in myself. The first few months were heaven. I had just completed four years as pastor of a church in a challenging setting, and now to do nothing but read and write felt like a wonderful vacation.

But then the Scottish winter rolled in, and it paralleled the gloom in my soul. Study was all I had to do — no preaching, no committee meetings, no lunches with elders, no hospital calls. Suddenly I realized the pastorate had not prepared me for disciplined study.

If the slightest feeling of boredom came over me, I had always had an escape: If reading a chapter of theology began to feel like slogging through knee-deep mud, well, there was always Mr. Smith to visit or a phone call to make or a luncheon to schedule. I discovered that as a pastor I could be busy in an undisciplined, even irresponsible way.

Yet discipline is required for all great endeavors. Louis Nizer, still a practicing attorney in his eighties, was asked if luck existed in trial law. He said yes, but added, "It only comes in the library at three o'clock in the morning. That holds true for me to this day. You'll find me in the library looking for luck at three o'clock in the morning." And that's probably where a lot of inspiration for ministry is found, too.

The movie *Field of Dreams* is a whimsical story about a young Iowa farmer who hears a voice in the cornfield say, "If you build it, he will come."

"Build what?" the farmer wants to know. A ball park, he learns. Who will come? Shoeless Joe Jackson, the Chicago White Sox legend. More importantly, another player will also come: the farmer's deceased father. So the farmer plows his corn under and marks out a diamond in the field. Sure enough, Shoeless Joe Jackson appears, along with seven other White Sox players and a few old New York Giants — and his father.

"If you build it, he will come." That's also true for the pastor. If we create the right conditions in our lives, our Father will more likely visit with the truth and inspiration needed to speak in his name.

It's not easy to plow an open space in the busyness of parish life. But here are two ways that have helped me.

● *Establish a routine of time and place.* Unless study is made a regular, habitual part of my schedule, it will constantly be postponed for lack of time. Study makes no imperious claims on me; it never importunes with pleas of desperation. Hospital calls, committee meetings, counseling sessions, staff problems, correspondence, telephone calls — these things elbow their way to the front of the line, extorting time by threatening to make me appear uncaring or irresponsible if I don't give way to their demands.

But study waits quietly, almost helplessly, like a doctor who can't get near a victim because of the frantic activity surrounding the scene of the accident. So when I'm wise, I clear a way for study, protecting it in every way possible.

The rhythm of my week has a predictable pattern: the first half is heavily administrative, with time given to staff and committees, and the latter half is reflective, with time for reading, writing, and sermon preparation. I find it helps to be specific on my calendar by writing phrases such as "Read von Balthasar on prayer" or "Get caught up on journals."

Then, when faced with requests for my time, I can say, "I'm sorry, I already have a commitment scheduled. May I see you next Monday afternoon?" It also helps me to think of study not as time alone — for that seems so selfish when purchased at the expense of saying no to individuals — but as time in company with my whole congregation. I imagine their faces, expectant with anticipation, waiting to hear what I've learned. And I remind myself that I won't be able to offer them anything of substance if I don't study.

Many pastors enjoy the benefit of annual study leaves. My own denomination requires congregations to grant at least two weeks a year (cumulative up to six weeks) for this purpose. In addition, some pastors are given extended sabbaticals after several years of service. I seize these opportunities for expanding mind and spirit whenever offered so that I can participate in conferences, continuing education courses at seminaries, travel, and more in-depth research.

But study leaves and sabbaticals are extraordinary events, only frosting on the cake of regular, disciplined study. My ministry must depend upon more frequent feedings of the mind.

• *Teach the congregation.* Once a routine is established, it should be made known. We've all heard the jibe about pastors working only one day a week. Before dismissing such nonsense, we ought to listen to it: it may indicate a genuine lack of understanding about what we do. If we were more intentional about telling our congregations how we organize our time — especially our study time — we might find them more supportive of our efforts.

I periodically mention from the pulpit my need to study; I make certain the staff understands I'm more available earlier in the week than later; I tell those who want to see me that Thursday and Friday are not good days because of sermon preparation. By now most of the congregation know they dare not call me on Friday unless it's a *serious* emergency.

God's Side of the Ravine

John Stott's metaphor of bridge building offers me a helpful way to organize my study time: on the one side, God, and on the other, humanity. I learn from both. Here's how I deepen my understanding of God.

• *Both forest and trees.* To communicate the Word of God to the world of humanity, I begin with the biblical text. To organize my time for this task, I remember the so-called hermeneutical circle: the whole Scripture interprets its various parts, and the various parts reveal its whole. I want my study, therefore, to be both general and particular; I plan for reflection on the forest and for detailed study of individual trees.

To keep myself thinking about the broad sweep of God's revelation, I try to read four chapters in the Bible each day.

Now, parts of it, I admit, bore me. So to keep from getting lost in the genealogies of Genesis or drowning in the blood sacrifices of Leviticus, I read in four different places. A pattern I have used with profit is Robert Murray McCheyne's *Bible Reading Calendar*, introduced to his Scottish congregation in 1842. The calendar begins the year at Genesis, Ezra, Matthew, and Acts (the four great beginnings), so at the end of the year, I've read the Old Testament once and the New Testament twice.

Staying with it every day can sometimes be difficult (especially if I skip a day because of an early morning breakfast and have to read eight chapters the next day). I feel it's necessary, though, for a clear view of the forest. I'm surprised continually how the various passages interact with each other and with my upcoming sermons; connections I would have never made jump out at me through this daily discipline.

In addition, I set aside a few hours each week (two to four) for theological reading not connected in any obvious way with sermon preparation. To study only for next Sunday leaves me wading in shallow waters, so to stay fit I swim in the depths by working through a volume of systematic theology.

Early in my ministry, I made a choice I haven't regretted, though it would probably cause despair for my seminary language professors: with study time so limited, I decided to spend it with Karl Barth rather than Hebrew vocabulary lists. Consequently, my reading knowledge of Hebrew rapidly died, and my Greek isn't too healthy (actually, it's in the intensive care unit). But I believe a growing ability to think theologically (with breadth and depth) has more than compensated for the deficiency.

Earl Palmer remembers a senior class dinner at Princeton Seminary in which George Buttrick challenged the future pastors by saying, "When you are at Coney Island, don't tell the people of the concession on the boardwalk about which they know; tell them of the mystery of the sea, about which they don't know." Palmer went on: "Don't read only what your people are reading. . . . Read what your people are not reading."

The books that deserve our attention, I believe, are primary sources; leave secondary sources to others. The best books are often not carried by the average Christian bookstore, but most merchants happily order them.

Having a panoramic view of the forest isn't enough; I don't really see its wonder until I've closely examined individual trees. For me, study of the particulars of Scripture happens as I prepare for sermons. I dissect the text, sentence by sentence, word by word, asking a thousand questions and trying to answer them myself before reading the commentaries.

I often find myself impatient, not wanting to stay with the text long enough. But I've learned that the best expositors, like Jacob wrestling with the angel, won't let it go until they get the blessing (and often a pain in the thigh, too).

Freeman Patterson, a professional photographer, has described the way he approaches his art: "On those frosty mornings when I grab my camera and tripod and head out into the meadow behind the house, I quickly forget about me. I stop thinking about what I'd do with the photographs, or about self-fulfillment, and lose myself in the sheer magic of rainbows in the grass."

The way Patterson surrenders himself to his subject is the way I like to become wholly captivated by a text. I find this difficult, however. Many things distract me before I'm finished seeing the text itself: possible sermon outlines, an idea to comfort the disturbed or to disturb the comfortable, a great story I've been saving for a dramatic illustration. These things — and a hundred more — can seize my attention as rabbits distract a hunting dog. But when I manage to keep my eyes focused on the pheasant, as it were, I end up with more to feed my people.

Only after I've spent time with the text itself do I let myself wander through the commentaries. And I mean wander. I don't feel compelled to read every word of every commentary in my library; I meander through them, checking my own exegesis to make sure I'm not being dishonest with the text and watching for ideas I might have missed. I try to read at least one historical/critical commentary and a couple of expositional/homiletical commentaries.

• *Dailies to quarterlies.* For the task of getting grounded on God's side of the ravine, there are many periodicals available to update us on recent theological trends, practical advice, book reviews, and news of the Christian world. These can be important resources stimulating our thinking and pointing to what God is doing in our world.

But I'm cautious with periodicals. They can consume a great deal of time, piling up and burying me in a truckload of guilt. So I scan periodicals, occasionally using the last half-hour at the office to get through the accumulated stack. When an article interests me, I slow down, perhaps copying it for my files.

Humanity's Side of the Ravine

My first task in study is to sink one side of the bridge deeply into the soil of God, the Word of God. But the bridge building isn't complete until the other pylon has been sunk deeply into the soil of humanity, the world. Here's how I do that.

• *Pay attention to people.* Exegeting Scripture isn't enough; I must also exegete human life. Often the people who drain my emotions and distract my thinking are important resources for study. I want to know those with whom I minister, not in the way a salesman knows a client well enough to make a sale but rather in the way a husband knows his wife, with a participatory knowledge that transforms him as much as it transforms her. I don't want my knowledge to be simply utilitarian, for that leads to manipulation; it must be incarnational, for that leads to transformation. I've found the best way to know people is to listen to them.

When Frank and John told me they both had AIDS, I found it difficult to silence my inner voices — judgmental voices, I'm sorry to admit — long enough to hear them. But I tried. I began to hear two stories of anguish. Frank had an identical twin brother who was also homosexual. Both Frank and John said they couldn't remember deliberately choosing this themselves. They lamented their impending deaths. And they spoke of their love for each other. Though I disagree with their lifestyle, that conversation moved me to compassion as I recognized the human dimension to the issue of homosexuality.

• *Reading to know our world.* Thankfully, my knowledge of humanity need not be limited by my circle of friends and parishioners. Through books I can enter into the lives of others.

Because reading time is precious, I'm careful about what I read. (I sometimes think I take as much time choosing what to read as I spend reading.) Every year publishers dump 50,000 new books on the market, and even if 49,000 aren't worth the paper they're printed on, that still leaves a good many crying for my attention.

In selecting books, I pay careful attention to reviews (my favorite weekly source is the *New York Times Book Review)* and recommendations from people I trust. Also, if I find an especially challenging and inspiring author, I read her other works, and then I read the thinkers who have influenced her. Good books, then, lead me to other good books.

My goal is to finish at least one book a week. This seems necessary to me, since I'm faced with the weekly task of preaching. I usually juggle four different books at once. In addition to the volume of theology I've already mentioned, I'm always in a novel and a biography. The fourth book shifts between different categories — most often social and political commentaries, religious works (not strictly theology), and psychology.

The daily newspaper consumes large amounts of time, and

for me it's rarely worth it, even though I receive one of the nation's finest. I limit my newspaper reading to the front page, occasional editorials, and a quick scan of the sports and arts sections. Most news develops over several days, so a weekly news magazine like *Time* or *Newsweek* offers a good summary. (For many years I've read *Time* cover to cover.)

• *The electronic media.* The people in our congregations, however, do not spend most of their time reading. Electronic media influence them far more than the printed page. The average American spends four-and-a-half hours each day watching television — an increase of 80 percent in the past fifteen years. If we're not watching some television, we're out of touch with an important part of today's world.

As for radio, I don't follow my natural inclinations and turn to the classical music station when I jump into the car. Many of my parishioners — perhaps most — prefer light rock to the music of Bach. So I have my dial set on a popular "top-forty" station and keep it there as long as my aesthetic sensibilities can take it. As with television, popular music reveals much about our contemporary culture. And besides, I've grown to like the beat.

• *Cultural events.* Most communities offer opportunities to experience movies, drama, concerts, and visual arts. Nowadays, even those in rural areas enjoy traveling performances; few pastors are completely cut off from these things. Time and money, of course, may limit taking full advantage of what's available. But when I do see a movie or watch a play or listen to a concert or visit a gallery, I often find my mind stretched and my emotions touched.

Recording What I Study

Unless a pastor has a perfect memory, storing and retrieving the fruit of our study will be necessary. Filing systems, I suppose, merit the comment C. S. Lewis made about the devil: the two great errors we make are to think too much or too little about them.

An elaborate system, complete with codes and cross-references and computer programs, can create a methodological legalism, causing me to join with the apostle Paul in crying, "Wretched man that I am! Who will deliver me from this body of death?"

But the stories, quotations, and images need to be recorded to be remembered. I keep with me at all times (except in the shower) a small hand-held recorder. It uses a microcassette, which can store 120 minutes of dictation. Many reasonably priced models are on the market, and I would consider myself horribly deprived without one. If the proverbial push came to shove, I would probably trade my entire set of Kittel or maybe even the *Church Dogmatics* for one.

When I come across something in my reading or have a thought I don't want to forget or think of an interesting image, I simply reach for my recorder and speak to my secretary, "Susie, a quotation card . . ." She will then type whatever I tell her on a four-by-six-inch card and add the appropriate bibliographic references I may want to keep.

Before using this method, I might have found something worth remembering, but an argument would immediately ensue: *I really should get up, get a piece of paper, and write this down; on the other hand, my shoes are off, my feet are up, and a tired man deserves to relax.* The treasure would never get recorded. Now I simply reach for my recorder, push a button, and in seconds it's accomplished.

What do I do with the cards? I do *not* file them, at least not immediately. I keep a pile growing for about a year, because a good quotation or illustration can almost always be used in a variety of contexts. Just after I've written a bare-bones sermon outline, during the brainstorming part of the preaching process, I shuffle through the stack. This doesn't take much time; after a few weeks, a card is so familiar that one glance reminds me of its content.

About once a year I force myself to categorize each card and file it according to a specific subject. Through the years the file boxes have accumulated. In the event of a fire, I would probably risk my life to carry them to safety before anything else.

Building the bridge between God and humanity requires disciplined study. The work isn't always easy, but we have no choice. The Lord deserves our minds as well as our hearts in his great enterprise.

Leonardo da Vinci was once hard at work on a great painting. It was nearly complete when suddenly he called a student to him, gave him the brush, and said, "You finish it."

The student protested, feeling unworthy.

But da Vinci said, "Will not what I have done inspire you to do your best?"

God's masterful work of creation and redemption through Jesus Christ inspires me to excel in the difficult task of enlarging the mind to expand the ministry.

All the permanent fruits and progress that result from our leadership are based on strong character.

— *Maxie Dunnam*

CHAPTER SEVEN

Strengthening Character

For several years our church has debated whether people should applaud after special music, especially in the 11:00 A.M. service. At a board meeting, someone caught me off guard by raising that issue out of nowhere.

For some reason it struck a nerve, and when I responded, my voice quivered and my blood pressure rose. "For anybody to criticize people who are responding to their feelings in worship," I snapped, "is as insensitive as anything I know."

Everyone in the room was taken back by my obvious anger. I

rarely lose control of my emotions.

Eventually I took the edge off the situation by stumbling into a humorous story: "Can Christians dance?" a man asked a preacher. "Some can," the preacher replied, "and some can't."

I finally said, "If people want to applaud, I think we're going to just have to accept that."

Emotional outbursts at a board meeting can be the beginning of the end of a pastor's ministry. That's one effect character has on a pastor's ministry. But of far greater importance are the permanent fruits and progress that result from our leadership based on character. Character gives authority. It makes a person an inspiring example for others and guides sound decisions. Character brings stability to one's life and ministry.

Those are some of the reasons I've continued to work on my character as I lead the people of God. And here are some of the principles I've learned in my journey.

Ministry Handicaps Character

Although the average parishioner thinks being a pastor makes it easier to grow in character, we know otherwise. Vocational ministry can dry and stiffen the red, tacky earth of the human spirit for several reasons.

• *Need for job security.* During the racial upheaval in Mississippi in the 1950s and '60s, I took a clear stand with the civil rights movement, which brought me into direct conflict with many in our church. At one point, the leaders held a special board meeting to confront the issue, with some deacons supporting and others opposing me.

After the meeting had gone on for some time, one opponent, who wielded substantial power in the church, asked, "Well now, what can we expect of you in the future?"

I replied, "You can expect me to be consistent with what I feel the gospel is calling me to do."

That was an intimidating moment, a situation in which I could have easily compromised for the sake of job security or the church budget. As I learned then, the church is no refuge from temptation.

• *Frequent moves.* This is a reality of many pastors' ministries. But when you move regularly, every two or three years, you can't clarify troubling issues or work through recurring problems.

One pastor I know of had a terrible temper. Invariably, within a year or two of beginning a new ministry, he'd end up shouting at a member or a transient or a staff person. He was never dismissed for such behavior, but neither was he able to work on it: he just kept moving from church to church. It never happened often enough in one church for people to begin to challenge him on it.

• *High expectations.* A story is told about a woman who approached the great Scottish preacher Alexander Whyte, complimented him profusely, and said, "Oh, Dr. Whyte, if I could just be as saintly as you are!"

"Madam," he replied. "If you could see into my heart, you would spit in my face."

We may fear that if people discover who we really are, we're finished, or at a minimum, our credibility and influence will wane. The human reflex is to hide, to put on a mask. Hypocrisy is the greatest temptation of religious professionals.

• *Stereotyping.* On the other hand, some people don't want us to be real saints, those who by word and deed call people to more Christlike behavior. They want us to be merely nice, fulfilling our role with reasonable skill and efficiency. Under that expectation, it's easy to become complacent. Instead of striving to become all that Christ calls us to be, we simply do what is expected of us: regular hospital calls, decent sermons, warm blessings at women's groups. Ministry is certainly that much, but not only that much.

• *Family pressures.* Although family pressures aren't unique to a minister's family, they are exacerbated by the pressures of ministry.

After six months of married life, my wife and I hit a watershed. I cherished the image of the perfect pastor and the perfect pastor's wife. Being an extremely insecure person, I put high performance demands on myself — and my wife. Growing up in my family, emotions and affection were not freely expressed. Jerry, on the other hand, came from an accepting and gracious, expressive and affectionate family.

One day Jerry let me know, rather forcefully, how angry she had become with all the expectations I had placed on her. I stalked out of the room, saying, "When you can discuss this like an adult, we'll continue the conversation!"

Those were tough times we had to work through, and having to struggle with my identity as a pastor made it tougher.

Taking Advantage of the Pastorate

Although ministry has its hazardous side in terms of character growth, it also offers unique opportunities. One is the freedom to schedule our time. When I use my calendar wisely, I can make the following practices part of my regular routine.

● *Examination of conscience.* That's what one tradition calls a nightly, intentional combing through the words, events, and deeds of the day to see where we have done well or fallen short. Some practice this daily; others periodically set aside a day for this exercise.

During this time, I ask myself three questions. First, *Am I growing?*

For instance, I want increasingly to practice tough love. The heart of my theology, and rightly so, has been grace, but in reaction to the rigid background in which I was raised, I tend to err on the side of love and acceptance. Sometimes I'm almost Pollyannish with people.

I've been realizing more clearly, though, that my love must also call people to holiness. Our culture is so tolerant that I'm not doing anybody a favor by downplaying obedience to Christ. So I want to grow in my ability to communicate to people that God is gracious but also calls us to something higher.

The second question I ask myself is *Do I want to change?* Am I self-satisfied, comfortable with the status quo? If I see that I have plateaued, I examine my motives and priorities.

It came to me recently that for over a year I had not personally participated in a growth group. For years this has been a priority for me, but for various reasons I had felt too busy to be involved recently. I even became a bit paranoid: What if someone questions me about *my* group? I soon found five couples to join Jerry and me in a weekly group.

Third, I ask, *How deep is my desire for holiness?* Some might think this superficial, but one way I discern my desire for holiness is by how I interact with people individually and in small groups. If I realize I've been doing most of the talking, or if I've been greeting most people after the service in a perfunctory way, waiting for someone "important" three or four places back in line, I know I'm losing my desire for holiness. One aspect of holiness is a loss of self-concern and an absorption in love and care of others. That demands total attention and is tested in everyday relationships.

• *Do the good.* Endless introspection is a potential pitfall for those who pursue growth. I have found that one safeguard is in Wesley's phrase, "Do all the good you can, and do no harm." Character results from both reflection and action. If we do Christ's deeds, we become like Christ; we develop character.

I find tremendous benefit from doing acts of mercy apart from explicit pastoral responsibilities — although it's my pastoral role that gives me entrée into so many acts of mercy. For instance, I've helped our church construct Habitat for Humanity homes, pounding nails at the job site. I've joined some of our church's mission teams to places like Costa Rica.

I don't do that just as an example for others; it's good for me — even though I keep thinking about the dozen things I should be doing more directly related to pastoral ministry!

The same idea underlies some of my scheduling policies. I have instructed my secretary that within the time I give to counseling each week, she should make appointments for *anyone* who asks — first come, first serve. I don't want her to screen people so that the only ones who see me are leaders or people who can help the church (and thereby me). Some say I am failing to make the best use of my time, but I feel it is the best use of my soul.

• *Forceful devotional reading.* In the process of researching and writing a book called *The Living Workbook of Prayer,* I discovered I could read mountains of literature on prayer but not pray. Even reading a great writer like Oswald Chambers, unless I am intentional about application, little will change in the way I live.

So I decided to slant my workbook to "force" people to pray. I simply opened chapters with a brief discussion of the meaning or purpose of prayer, and then I asked the reader to practice prayer: e.g., to emphasize one aspect of prayer each day (intercession, praise, etc.). In other words, everything pointed to application.

I have kept that application-driven perspective in my own devotional reading since. Instead of ending a reading by simply closing the book or marveling at the prose or the thought, I ask myself questions: *What does this say about my emotions? My speech? My relationships? My family? My money?*

• *Turn your sermons on yourself.* For example, one Sunday in Advent, I took four Christmas hymns, like "To Whom Jesus Comes" and "O Come, O Come, Emmanuel," and preached about Christ coming into our lives. One point was that he comes to those who have everything or think they have everything.

I used that point to examine my own life. I realized, for instance, that I'm someone who has everything, at least what we usually mean by "everything": good health, financial security, career success. Also, I've been so busy with ministry at certain times that I've failed to communicate to my loved ones how important they are to me, how my ministry and my pastoral success mean little to me compared to their presence in my life. In fact, as a result of this sermon, I spent some time with my grown son trying to tell him just that.

Getting the Community Involved

One of our ministers does a great job at getting people involved in missions work. As a result of his commitment and example, many young couples from our church visit prisons or serve breakfast in shelters for the homeless. Their example, in turn, helps others take more seriously their discipleship.

Community is one of the greatest forces for building character, giving us models of obedience, holding us accountable, urging us to deal with things we would rather avoid, and supporting and loving us through tough times.

I've found my own growth in character to be inseparable from my relationships. Here, then, are various ways I integrate others into my life.

• *Creating a congregation that will help.* I've been the founding pastor of three congregations. I've discovered that each congregation develops its own personality, and in a new church that personality has a lot to do with the character of the pastor's ministry. Although this is less true in an established church, the pastor can shape a church's character by his character.

So one thing I regularly think about is what type of congregation I want to produce. What kind of community will help people, me included, grow? If I want to be a part of an unselfish, generous people, I can have some bearing on helping a congregation becoming unselfish and generous.

I want to be part of a community of people who care for one another. Consequently, more than anything else, I want people to know that I care about them. Even in a large congregation like the one I now serve, I try to institute ways to communicate that. My wife and I, for instance, have every person who joins the church in our home soon after they've joined.

I don't mean I get to know all these people personally. It's just one small way that I try to create the sense that we are a church who wants to be in relationship to one another. That, in the long run, helps create that kind of community. And that kind of community is one I need to grow in.

• *Finding a close circle.* The recovery movement has a lot to teach us about growing in character. And some of their main principles — honesty, confession, acknowledging dependence on God, living one day at a time — are best reinforced in small groups. I have found these principles useful in my own growth.

So I've been a part of peer groups: some have met weekly for twelve weeks; others have met until the group disbands of its own accord. I've found it difficult to meet with peers of different denominations: we've never been able to clarify our agenda, nor have we been able to be honest enough to make the group work. And to me, that's the key: mutual honesty and accountability.

Often that type of relationship can be established with one other clergy person. One of my best friends in Memphis is an Episcopal priest. Although we disagree theologically in a lot of ways, I share with him some of my personal struggles.

● *Public honesty.* In order to foster the desire for community in the church and in myself, I find it helpful to share from the pulpit some of my struggles. For example, I might tell the story of losing my temper with the board. I know one minister who told his congregation how he broke his knuckle: he lost his temper with his wife and put his fist through a wall — right where a stud ran!

Openness about my discipleship encourages me to keep striving in Christ. When I tell the church of my failures or goals, I feel a social (and "holy") pressure to not let people down. It also helps the congregation see that character growth requires patience and honesty.

Naturally, I'm discreet about what I share. And sometimes, we don't have to say much for the congregation to get the point. I know one pastor whose daughter is recovering from chemical addiction. The congregation knows about the situation, but he doesn't talk about it publicly. But he often will mention in sermons the pain of family problems; that's enough for his congregation to know that he knows whereof he speaks.

● *Paying attention to people.* I need community because I need to see the example of others doing the work of Christ. It's inspiring sometimes. But for me to be so helped, I've got to listen when people talk to me, and I've got to notice the good they do. Fortunately, in some cases it's pretty obvious.

Pauline Holworth, a woman in our congregation, is clearly a spiritual giant. Early in life she linked up with Frank Laubach and began to teach literacy, especially the each-one, teach-one method. It's been the most effective literacy tool in the world. She became his principle agent in the southeastern United States.

But rather than live on her laurels, now at age 85, she continues her sacrificial labors. Every Wednesday she visits Parchman Prison in Mississippi, one of the worst prisons in the country, about one hundred miles away. She teaches prisoners to read and write. She prays with and witnesses to them.

● *Letting church leaders help.* I've tried to build relationships with church leaders so that we can be open with one another. Apparently it's worked, because recently our staff parish committee, which has oversight of the staff, met with me to express concern about my work style. They felt I had not been giving enough time to myself and my family.

They were right, and their concern prompted me to adjust my hectic schedule as soon as possible. I know that if I don't make time for a Sabbath, my character will eventually be undermined by fatigue.

● *Drawing upon the family.* Early in my marriage, I was not willing to talk with my wife, Jerry, about my spiritual growth — frankly I was embarrassed by my lack of it. So I wouldn't insist that she go with me to retreats. My rationale was, *Well, that's not for her.*

But I was so insecure in my own spiritual growth, so concerned about my ministerial image, I couldn't open myself to her. We finally became mature enough to realize that if we didn't call upon one another for help, we were missing a tremendous resource.

Jerry now has given me significant feedback on several occasions. I mentioned earlier my becoming involved in a growth group. Jerry significantly contributed to that move. I had been urging people in our church to join growth groups while not being involved myself. In a noncensorious way, she advised me, "You can't tell everyone else to be in groups and not be involved yourself. That's going to cripple your integrity in the long run."

Keeping at It

Growth takes effort and time. It diverts us from "pastoral duties." We sometimes think, *If parishioners are satisfied with their pastor being a nice guy and minding the shop, why not be content with that?* Three reminders motivate me to stay at it.

- *It builds credibility.* I eventually left the church in which some of the leaders chided me for my involvement in civil rights issues. But a year after I left, I received a call from the man who was my chief critic. He was phoning me from 2,000 miles away because his son was in trouble, and the man wanted to talk. I was gratified that he saw in me more than someone who was "too involved in social issues."

- *It's where ministry begins and ends.* I've read about and experienced the latter in my own life:

When we start in ministry, we're enthusiastic for God, and we want nothing more than to be sterling men and women of God.

Whether it's due to our seminary training or ecclesiastical machinery or competition among pastors, early on we're tempted to become increasingly preoccupied with success. We start climbing the ladder, looking for a bigger church, a bigger salary, and greater recognition.

Later in ministry, we realize how we've strayed. It's not that we've ignored character completely, but we have not had the time or inclination to concern ourselves with it. In our forties and fifties, though, we return to putting emphasis on our relationship with God.

Whenever I get distracted from that, I remember my first love, and what will, in the end, be my last love.

- *It's what God is finally interested in.* A young priest complained to Mother Theresa about all the demands being put upon him and how it was taking away from his ability to serve the poor, which was his life's passion.

She responded, "Your vocation is not to serve the poor. Your vocation is to love Jesus."

My vocation is not, ultimately, to serve the church. My vocation is to love Jesus. That's what I want, with all my heart. Character emerges out of such a heart.

Our bodies have rhythms, and these must be honored in order to maintain fitness for ministry.
                                          — *Donald McCullough*

CHAPTER EIGHT
Becoming Fit for Ministry

One Memorial Day I had intended to go for a run along the beach about noon, but by late morning I had developed a backache. *Probably just stress,* I thought. So instead of exercising, I lay down for a nap. Twenty minutes later I was writhing and whimpering like a dog that had just had its hindquarters squashed along the highway. Some demon of torture was flaying my insides with a dull, ragged-edged knife.

A green blur of medical efficiency quickly discovered the cause of my anguish: a kidney stone, wearing hobnail boots, was kicking the bejabbers out of my ureter. Certain words, such as "kidney stone," are devoid of all meaning until you experience them. Some readers of this account will understand; the rest should immediately drop to their knees and thank God for blessed ignorance.

That afternoon I was not a spiritual man. I wish I could report that I praised God for doctors and hospitals, that I prayed for other sufferers around me, that I took comfort in the communion of saints, that I felt the peace that passes all understanding. But the closest thing to a "depth experience" came when they wheeled me into the emergency room and my morning breakfast rocketed up from my depths onto a waiting nurse. *Great entrance,* I thought, *I just hope she isn't a member of my church.*

My body was broken, and thus *I* was broken. A part of me felt compelled to be upbeat and spiritual about the whole affair, but frankly, the pain was too great to get very spiritual. I discovered afresh that day a key element in biblical theology: by God's design, our physical and spiritual lives cannot be separated; what happens to the one affects the other.

God has so structured things that creation moves with certain rhythms: night and day, seed time and harvest, life and death. Our bodies, too, have rhythms, and these must be honored in order to maintain fitness for ministry.

Francis Gary Powers, the pilot who was shot down over the Soviet Union spying for the United States, later became a traffic helicopter pilot in Los Angeles. In 1977 he and his partner were reporting on large canyon fires. Absorbed in this task, they failed to pay attention to their fuel gauge. The helicopter crashed just two miles from the airport, taking the lives of both men.

It's easy to get preoccupied with immediate responsibilities to the neglect of crucially important matters. It can cost not only productivity in ministry but our very lives. Certain rhythms we dare not disregard.

Work and Play

Pastoral work can be tiring; some days opening junk mail

seems too much to bear. Every job has its problems, of course, but for the most part, being a pastor provides a deeply satisfying way to make a living. To do things that matter, to serve the Lord and other people, to have flexibility and variety in scheduling — these are a few of the reasons why most of us wouldn't want to do anything else. Thus our work itself can be an important source of bodily health.

Consider the alternative. A Gallup Report published in 1984, *Religion in America,* cited a Johns Hopkins study that revealed a 1 percent increase in unemployment "is accompanied by an increase of 37,000 deaths — including 27,000 fatal cardiovascular cases, 650 murders, and 920 suicides — plus 4,000 additional admissions to state mental hospitals and 3,300 more criminals sentenced to prison." *Not* to work can be deadly.

But work must be regularly balanced with plenty of play. This isn't easy. Work — especially when it's satisfying — dons the regal robes of Importance and tyrannizes everything else. Play seems too small a thing to approach the throne with a request for time. In 1973 the average American enjoyed 26.2 hours of leisure each week; by 1987 the hours shrank to 16.6. Work will consume all it can get.

Perhaps this is why God commanded at least one day of play out of seven. It takes the hard edge of a commandment to cut back the ever-expanding encroachments of work. A divine suggestion wouldn't have stood a chance. As it is, the commandment barely gets a hearing.

I know: the Bible calls for a Sabbath *rest*, not a Sabbath play. But what is rest? I don't think it comes with doing nothing. Winston Churchill, in a marvelous essay about the pleasures of painting, put it this way:

"Change is the master key. A man can wear out a particular part of his mind by continually using it and tiring it, just in the same way as he can wear out the elbows of his coat. There is, however, this difference between the living cells of the brain and inanimate articles: one cannot mend the frayed elbows of a coat by rubbing the sleeves or shoulders, but the tired parts of the mind can be rested and strengthened, not merely by rest but by using other parts.

"It is not enough merely to switch off the lights that play upon the main and ordinary field of interest; a new field of interest must be illuminated. It is no use saying to the tired 'mental muscles' — if one may coin such an expression — 'I will give you a good rest,' 'I will go for a long walk,' or 'I will lie down and think nothing.' The mind keeps busy just the same. If it has been weighing and measuring, it goes on weighing and measuring. If it has been worrying, it goes on worrying. It is only when new cells are called into activity, when new stars become the lord of the ascendant, that relief, repose, refreshment are afforded."

I suggest we think of Sabbath rest as a time of God-ordained play. Play has two elements — freedom and delight. We play when, freed from the necessity of work, we do something for the sheer joy of it.

The center of Christian play is worship. What is praise but delight in God? Having been set free by grace, we enjoy the presence of God, playing as children with a Father in a holy game of love. With worship at the heart of play and play at the heart of worship, all play is lifted in importance. We may not demean this gift. To build a model train layout or fly a glider or scuba dive — to do these things for no other reason than pure delight — is to do something holy, something that witnesses to the Sabbath rest we have in Christ.

Play can be corrupted by turning it into work, by turning it into a means rather than enjoying it as an end. As a runner, I know the temptation to ruin this most childlike sport through an excessive focus on competition; getting better and better times, or running farther and farther, becomes more important than the joy of running itself. This "play," then, becomes a disguised form of work. The authenticity of play can always be judged by standards of freedom and delight. Here's the test: Does play bring out the child in me?

Put in my hand the rudder of a responsive boat, with a stiff wind in the sails and a bit of water breaking over the bow — it may not be heaven, but it's mighty close. My daughter often goes with me, and she knows the ritual on the way to the boat: we put '60s rock 'n' roll on the car stereo, roll down all the windows, and sing as loudly as possible, happily serenading other motorists on the freeway. By the time I get to the boat, I'm a little boy again. Nothing else matters. We laugh; we wave at other sailors and yell at motor-boaters; we eat plenty of junk food; I always philosophize about poetry in the soul of true sailors and other nonsense. I play, in other words, and it's something I desperately need to balance my work as a busy pastor.

Fast and Feast

Another important rhythm has to do with the fuel we feed our bodies to keep going. Food, like other good gifts from God, must be utilized wisely and kept in its proper place.

The biblical pattern of eating swung between the fast and the feast. Fasting, the abstinence of food, was a sign of repentance and utter dependence on God. Feasting, no less a spiritual discipline, was a sign of the goodness of God. Though most of the Israelites' meals were no doubt simple fare, they knew both seasons of absti-nence and the festivals of indulgence (the three most significant being Unleavened Bread, Weeks, and Booths).

This rhythm is also important today to maintain fitness for ministry. I view my own pattern of eating as falling along a con-tinuum: At one end, the occasional fast (for me, this has always been a spiritual discipline, though there is evidence suggesting the health benefits of occasionally cleansing our bodies through absti-nence); at the other end, the feasts in which I happily indulge myself with gratitude for the wonder of taste and the joy of good food. In between, I strive to be on the fast side of the continuum.

I'm no expert on nutrition, but through reading and listening to others more knowledgeable, I've come to some convictions about a healthy diet:

● I try to have a diet low in fat (a major factor in increasing the risk of heart disease and also the last calories in the body to be digested) and high in vegetables, fruits, and grains.

● Cutting down on fat, I eat more fish and chicken than beef. I'm not a purist; sometimes I simply must have a juicy hamburger or a sausage pizza (I like to think pizza is one of the major food groups). But I'm trying to lower substantially my intake of red meats.

- I go easy on desserts, certainly not forsaking them entirely, but most days of the week limiting myself to low-fat items like ginger snaps or graham crackers.

- I generally have a glass of wine with my dinner. In an era when alcoholism rages at epidemic proportions, a good case can be made for abstinence. But it may also be important to witness to the biblical principle of moderation. I am persuaded by a good deal of medical evidence that a daily glass of wine helps keep the arteries elastic and cleansed of plaque. (The French, for example, consume significantly more wine than Americans and have a much lower incidence of heart disease; some scientists see a positive relationship between these two facts.)

- I try to eat in moderate proportions and almost never eat between meals.

- I drink lots of water. During my kidney stone ordeal, the doctor told me I needed fifteen glasses a day. I don't always achieve that, but I try. Not only does water prevent dehydration, it cleanses the system. In cold and flu season, I'm especially careful to drink as much as possible.

- I take both a multiple vitamin and vitamin C. Doctors say this is unnecessary if one eats balanced meals, but I can't be sure I do every day. As a precaution, therefore, I take these supplements. I also believe in the benefits of extra vitamin C. I'm fully aware of the scientific disagreement concerning this, but since the body sloughs off what it doesn't use of this vitamin, I've decided it can't hurt. Besides, though it may be nothing but a placebo, I nevertheless feel it helps.

So much for my usual eating patterns. With no guilt at all, I occasionally move over to the feast side of the continuum. The great banquet, after all, was Jesus' central image of the coming kingdom of God. A well-prepared meal, offered up in love and savored in gratitude, is a great gift, a foretaste of the marriage supper of the Lamb.

Robert Farrar Capon, perhaps with some exaggeration, has commented on our current fear of eating: "Food these days is often identified as the enemy. Butter, salt, sugar, eggs are all out to get you. And yet at our best we know better. Butter is . . . well, butter: it glorifies almost everything it touches. Salt is the sovereign perfecter of all flavors. Eggs are, pure and simple, one of the wonders of the world. And if you put them all together, you get not sudden death but hollandaise — which in its own way is not one bit less a marvel than the Gothic arch, the computer chip, or a Bach fugue. Food, like all the other triumphs of human nature, is evidence of civilization — of that priestly gift by which we lift the whole work into the exchanges of the Ultimate City, which even God himself longs to see it become" (Robert Farrar Capon, *The Supper of the Lamb*, 1989).

Well, Capon's enthusiasm may have overstated the case a bit, but he has a point. While we ought to eat simply and sensibly, spending most of the time on the fast side of the continuum, once in a while we not only may but ought to move over toward the feast side. This is the biblical rhythm, after all. One of my friends eats sparingly all week long, but on the weekends lets herself eat anything she wants. Another never eats dessert, except on Thursday evening, and then anything goes. The details will vary according to individual nutritional needs and tastes, but what should be the same for all is a rhythm.

Rest and Exercise

With the exception of an occasional run up a flight of hospital stairs because of slow elevators, pastoring is a sedentary lifestyle. We sit at desks, sit in counseling sessions, sit in committee meetings, and sit in living rooms. Except for the half-hour we stand in the pulpit, most of our job happens sitting down.

The importance of an exercise program, therefore, cannot be overestimated. It is widely agreed that our bodies stay healthier with regular exercise. Charles Spurgeon once said, "Our hearts like muzzled drums are beating funeral marches to the grave." Yes, but as we periodically increase the speed of our heartbeat, we slow down the march. Aerobic exercise (activity that steps up the heartbeat) strengthens our cardiovascular system, thereby decreasing the chances of heart disease and often increasing our overall physical well-being.

The point of exercise is not to become a hunk in the pulpit. About a year ago an elder in my congregation insisted that I visit his health club. I had been having minor calf pain, which had interfered with my running for a few weeks. He thought this was the answer.

Eventually I ran out of excuses and met him there on a Saturday morning. The place was no "fun family fitness center"; it was filled with hardcore, serious weightlifters (the first person I met was "Iron Mike," who had the biggest tattoo-covered arm I've ever seen). The owner of the gym put me through the paces, demonstrating more pieces of equipment than could have been found in a medieval torture chamber. The next morning I was so sore I couldn't lift my hands for the benediction. I decided not to become a preaching Arnold Schwarzenegger. I have no idea why God created some muscles, but I know I don't need every one of mine to be bulging.

What I do need, however, is cardiovascular exercise. So for the last eighteen years I've been a runner. I began with a modest one mile jog, soon increasing that to two miles. Four years after starting, we moved to Edinburgh for my Ph.D. work, and the Scottish countryside provided a wonderful diversion from Karl Barth and Dietrich Bonhoeffer. I experimented with increasing my mileage; before long I was running seven miles every day, even in the winter. I felt pretty virtuous, but my knees began to hurt. So after a couple of years, I cut back to every other day and found my body felt much better. For the last ten years I have run six miles on Monday, Wednesday, Friday (sometimes), and Saturday.

Not only has this exercise kept my body in good condition, it has done at least as much for my emotions and spirit. I would run even if there were no physical benefits, for it makes me *feel* better. It's a great change of pace, a great release of tension, a great way to daydream and free my mind for creative thoughts. Sometimes I think it's my most productive part of the day; sermon outlines often fall into place, articles take shape, and programmatic ideas well up from subconscious depths. All of this is a by-product, the natural result of exercise.

Researchers have demonstrated that during vigorous exercise our bodies create endorphins (chemicals similar to morphine), which are produced in the brain and pituitary gland. Researchers from Massachusetts General Hospital took blood samples from volunteers before and after exercise, and they discovered that after two months of workouts the subjects' endorphin levels were up 145 percent following an hour of exercise. Endorphins apparently block pain signals to the brain and stimulate the parts of the brain associated with elation and pleasure.

Not everyone can run, of course. For some, running ranks only slightly higher than a poke in the eye with a sharp stick. Other ways of increasing cardiovascular activity include brisk walking, swimming, bicycling, hiking, tennis — any activity that gets the heart ticking faster and forces deeper breathing will pay significant health dividends.

Here are a few suggestions for beginning an exercise program:

● Before beginning a new regimen, get a physical examination from your family doctor. Make sure everything works well and will not be harmed by stress.

● Start slowly. Many people begin exercising with a burst of enthusiasm and soon burn out. Take your time. My cardiovascular capacity increased more rapidly than my muscles and tendons could take. A wise doctor slowed me down, told me to take my time increasing my speed and distance, and it made all the difference.

● Be realistic. You don't need to run the Boston Marathon next year. Twenty minutes of aerobic exercise three days a week is enough for most people. According to statistical evidence, the health benefits beyond that are minimal.

Exercise is important for good health. But too much physical activity can be harmful. Our bodies need the rhythm of exercise and rest; they need a period of recovery from the strain of exertion. Vigorous workouts cause small injuries to muscles and tendons and joints, and it takes about forty-eight hours for these to heal. I find it best, therefore, to schedule time for rest.

Up and Down

According to pollster Lou Harris, 86 percent of Americans are chronically stressed out. That number, no doubt, includes pastors.

In fact, if pastors alone were surveyed, the percentage might be even higher. Think about it: we must preach truth in love, boldly enough to get through the defenses of our hearers and graciously enough to keep from getting run out of town; we must take a telephone call from someone threatening suicide, just as we're leaving the office to speak to a denominational gathering; we must find the patience to speak (once more!) to a terribly needy and insecure person; we must lead a congregation that often demands more than we have to give, and yet cope with our own personal and family problems. An air traffic controller at O'Hare airport cannot have more stress!

Not all stress is bad. The only ones who have absolutely no stress live in coffins. Hans Selye, the father of stress research, said, "No one can live without experiencing some degree of stress. You may think that only serious disease or intensive physical or mental injury can cause stress. This is false. Crossing a busy intersection, exposure to a draft, or even sheer joy are enough to activate the body's stress mechanism to some extent. Stress is not even necessarily bad for you; it is also the spice of life, for any emotion, any activity, causes stress."

But stress is healthy only if short-lived. Bodily systems activate, for example, for the challenge of playing a championship softball game, but after the third out in the bottom of the ninth inning, the excitement has passed. Stress becomes dangerous over a long period of time, when the body stays up and doesn't come down.

What makes sustained stress dangerous is the continued presence of adrenalin. Our bodies produce this hormone to prepare us for emergency situations, to enable the fight-or-flight response. Adrenalin helps activate heart muscles, sends glucose to the muscles, raises blood pressure, and increases the heart rate. But too much adrenalin causes damage.

Archibald Hart, dean of the graduate school of psychology at Fuller Theological Seminary, has written a helpful book on the subject of stress: *Adrenalin & Stress* (Word, 1991). He points out that a chronic increased flow of adrenalin produces serious consequences, including:

- An increase in the production of blood cholesterol,

- A narrowing of the capillaries and other blood vessels that can shut down the blood supply to the heart,

- A decrease in the body's ability to remove cholesterol,

- An increase in the blood's tendency to clot,

- An increase in the depositing of plaque on the walls of the arteries.

"The adrenalin keeps the system moving at a high speed," writes Hart, "and deterioration occurs at a faster rate. We actually age faster." In other words, stress can kill.

Hart suggests ways in which we can manage the adrenalin level in our system and thus control the effects of stress. Here are a few things I have learned from him.

1. Plan to be down. After high adrenalin arousal, it's important to let ourselves fall into a state of low arousal. Unfortunately, this doesn't feel very good. Actually, it can feel like the bottom of the bird cage. When adrenalin drops, we feel low until our bodies reach a new state of equilibrium. "Blue Monday" has a biological cause!

I used to keep myself active on Sunday afternoons. Perhaps I was afraid of the crash, or perhaps I thought it would be too unspiritual to be depressed after experiencing the Lord's blessing. After preaching in three worship services, I would take a brief nap and then hustle off to the tennis court or some other activity. But I heard Hart, in a workshop for pastors, tell how he plans for periods of depression after speaking engagements. When he speaks out of town, he asks to be taken to the airport a few hours early, finds a quiet corner in the terminal, and lets the depression break over him like waves. By allowing this to happen, he said, his system more quickly gets back to normal.

So I tried it. I no longer struggle to keep my emotions from falling into the pit. (One Sunday after lunch I said to my family, "Excuse me, I'm going to the bedroom to feel lousy.") By Sunday evening I have almost no positive feelings left; I feel lonely, useless, disinterested in everything, a failure. This is not fun. But I discovered something interesting: the low periods pass more quickly. On

Mondays I usually feel great, ready to charge forward into another week. (Before, when I held off the depression, it would hit more fiercely about Wednesday.)

After periods of stress, plan for a necessary drop in emotions. Depression is not always an enemy; it may be an ebb and flow essential for good health.

2. Enjoy the pause that refreshes. Hart writes: "Of all the techniques available for counteracting stress and reducing the symptoms of distress, deliberate relaxation represents the most well-developed and thoroughly researched. . . . Not only is it the cheapest healing force we know of, it is probably the most effective. Believe me, relaxation is a powerful tool." Periods of intentional relaxation — daily and weekly — can help reduce the negative effects of stress in our lives.

Hart mentions several well-known techniques: stretching and relaxation of muscles, deep breathing, reminding oneself that God still sits on the throne. One of his suggestions, though, was new to me: hand warming. Adrenalin causes the blood to flow to the vital organs; this leaves the extremities colder than usual. You can actually warm your hands — and thereby reverse the flow of blood and ease the stress — by imagining them in hot water, say, or resting on the warm sand at the beach.

When I first heard this, I thought to myself, *Sure.* But biofeedback on my own body proved it. The temperature of my hands rose as I visualized (and tried to feel) them in hot water. I discovered I have more control over my bodily systems than I thought!

The point is, plan for relaxation; schedule it into each day and week. On Fridays I write my sermons. At about ten o'clock, I go for a little walk around the church campus. I breathe deeply, thank God for my congregation, stretch and relax my muscles. The rest of the morning goes much better.

3. Sleep it off. When adrenalin is up, sleep diminishes. But with increased sleep, the body more easily recovers from the effects of elevated adrenalin. Sleep is a primary way to heal the damage caused by stress.

Hart's research on sleep stunned me: "It is my belief that for good stress-disease prevention, the average adult needs between eight and ten hours of sleep each night, with some going as high as eleven hours. Some individual differences (such as age, lifestyle, and physical health) will vary the actual amount needed, but an average of nine hours seems to offer the best protection, according to my clinical experience. Under conditions of high stress, the apparent need for sleep may diminish, and extra sleep should be provided as soon as the stress period is over. If the stress demand continues, then extra 'rest' time should be provided even if sleep is not possible. I am convinced that most of us could improve our physical and emotional health dramatically if we just slept or rested a little longer than we usually do in our highly driven culture."

I do not get as much sleep as Hart recommends, but I do plan for more sleep during seasons of stress. I've never been able to sleep late; I'm always up with the earliest bird. So when I need more sleep, I try to minimize evening meetings and go to bed earlier. It helps. When I have both high-level stress and inadequate sleep, I get more frazzled, more easily irritated. The sleep seems to restore energies deep within.

Laughter and Tears

For many years *Reader's Digest* has had a section titled, "Laughter Is the Best Medicine." Whether it's the *best* depends upon your ailment, I suppose, but it's certainly a good medicine for much of what ails us.

Laughter puts things in perspective: humor springs from the incongruities and ironies that afflict our humanity. Ben Patterson tells the apocryphal story of Bill Russell, the legendary center for the Boston Celtics: "If it isn't true, it ought to be. According to the story, he was in the midst of an intense basketball game when, as he ran down court, he burst out laughing. The laughter grew until he had to stop playing and just lean over, his hands on his knees, and guffaw.

"Coach Red Auerbach called time out and screamed for his seemingly mad center to come over to the sideline. 'What on earth are you laughing about?' demanded Auerbach. 'You could lose the game for us, you know!'

"It took Russell a few moments to regain his composure and explain, 'Well you see, it suddenly hit me — here I am running around in my underwear in front of thousands of people, trying to throw a little ball through a hoop, and I'm getting paid to do it!' "

Every now and then a similar thing happens to me on Sunday mornings. *Here I am*, I think to myself, *all dressed up in my fancy pulpit robe, sounding so sure of myself, speaking in God's name — and I'm really nothing but a scared little kid who can barely keep his act together from day to day*. It's enough to make me laugh, when I think about it.

Laughter isn't simply good for the spirit, it's good for the body. In 1964 Norman Cousins, long-time editor of *Saturday Review*, was diagnosed as having a serious collagen disease; his bodily tissues were literally coming apart, and he was told he wouldn't live long. He didn't believe doctors had a right to say when someone was going to die, so he started treating himself.

A significant part of his program called for laughter. He wondered whether positive emotions would create a healthier chemical balance in his body. So he watched old *Candid Camera* and Marx brothers films. It worked. He said, "I made the joyous discovery that ten minutes of genuine belly laughter had an anesthetic effect and would give me at least two hours of pain-free sleep." Cousins, not incidentally, lived and went on to become a senior lecturer at the UCLA School of Medicine.

Laughter may be more important for health than we realize. It certainly helps me. I once had a presbytery executive who would occasionally telephone me: "Don, this pastor dies, meets St. Peter at the Golden Gate. . . ." We would laugh together, and then he would say, "That's all, goodbye." He was a wise pastor to pastors! We have a telephone prayer chain at our church; call in your concern, and it's conveyed through the congregation. Perhaps we should also have a joke chain: call in your good ones, and pass them around for mutual well-being.

But we need more than laughter. To maintain fitness for ministry we must also know the joy of tears. The ability to cry is a blessing from God we dare not neglect. Unfortunately, many of us — particularly males — have lost it through disuse. Our North

American culture discourages men from crying; tears, we have been conditioned to believe, are a sign of weakness ("Be a big boy, Johnny, and stop crying").

A study conducted by a psychiatric nurse at Marquette University indicates that women cry five times as much as men. This study of 128 men and women demonstrates a close link between regular crying and good health (which may be one reason women, on the average, live longer than men).

I'm trying to learn from women. For many, many years I didn't shed a single tear. I wasn't consciously holding back; my plumbing just didn't seem to work. But one day a flash flood hit. During a time of great stress, a tightness gathered in my chest, a pressure increased until I thought I would explode. Instead, to my complete astonishment, torrents of tears burst from undammed ducts. I let it rip: I moaned and groaned, beat my fist on the desk, and made a first-class mess of my shirt.

It felt great. It was as though a storm had passed through me, leaving a peaceful calm. A marvelous tranquility settled on my spirit. And then I wondered why I had allowed this gift to fall into such disrepair. The ability to cry, so far as I know, was granted only to humans — humans made in the image of the God who became flesh in Jesus, a man who cried. I had learned the verse in Sunday school, the shortest verse in the Bible: "Jesus wept." If the one who revealed not only true God but true humanity cried, why should I be afraid of tears?

I'm still not good at it. Three or four times a year, I have a mild session of weeping; only about once a year do I cut loose with a wailing, Kleenex-demolishing session. But I'm getting better, and I have found it an important part of keeping fit for ministry.

Work and play, fast and feast, rest and exercise, up and down, laughter and tears: these are important rhythms for the health of body, mind, emotions, spirit — and ministry.

Part Four
Redeeming
the Time

Determining God's call usually involves a prosaic wrestling with who we are and where we are placed.
— *Donald McCullough*

Time for Things That Matter

"It is finished."

According to John, these were the last words of Jesus. But what exactly was finished?

He was but a young man with many years of ministry ahead of him. He had been preaching for only three years and had little to show for it: the last of his followers had fled in fear; the kingdom of Rome seemed in no way threatened by the kingdom of God; recovery of sight hadn't yet come to many of the blind; captives were still doing time; liberty had not yet come to the underside of society.

Nothing much was finished, except that which God had called Jesus to do. "I glorified you on earth," Jesus prayed, "by finishing the work that you gave me to do."

It must have been tempting for him to try to do more, to try to, well, save the world. A few more years and who knows? Perhaps thousands more could be exposed to the kingdom's message; at least hundreds more could be touched by its healing power.

If he were like most of us, he would have let Peter go through with his rescue attempt — anything to get back to ministry, to continue the work. To the end though, he refused to take responsibility for everything — to do what really mattered. For that reason, he *did* save the world.

Every pastor must ask, *What am I called to do? Where should I invest my time and energies? What should I seek as a goal?* Here are some principles I keep in mind as I seek to answer these questions.

Hearing God in Person and Place

Sometimes I wish God would use the telephone. I imagine an angelic voice saying, "Is this Don McCullough? Please stand by. God would like a word with you." And then a voice, sounding like eternity and filled with wisdom and authority and love would say, "Don, I want you to lead your congregation in a four million dollar capital fund campaign." No uncertainty, no ambivalence.

And on my part, there would be single-minded obedience — or so I imagine. Actually, I would probably wonder if it had really been God on the line, and I would equivocate in my response as thoroughly as when I read a clear word of Scripture. But it's hard not wishing for such clear, concrete guidance.

Determining God's call usually involves a more prosaic wrestling with two factors: We come to understand what God wants us to do by evaluating *who* we are and *where* we are placed.

We begin with self-evaluation — an honest assessment of our gifts and interests and joys and discomforts — because the commissioning God is none other than the creator God. The God who sends has already equipped us. True, God sometimes surprises, using apparently unlikely candidates as instruments of his will. But for the most part, we may rationally evaluate our natural talents and inclinations, and this will be the first (probably most important) step toward discovering God's will for our lives.

For me to pray about becoming a denominational executive, say, would indicate less spirituality than stupidity. Committee meetings remind me of vaccination shots: necessary at times, but tolerable only in moderation. Denominational executives go from one meeting to the next like drunks hitting every bar in town, and for the most part, they remain sober and, more importantly, productive for the kingdom. And that only increases my incomprehension at how they manage to get through each day. I praise God for those so constituted; I know I'm not made that way, and there's no sense keeping this one on my prayer list.

Here's my general rule: unless struck by lightning, I assume that what God wants of me will be consistent with how he created me. So I pay attention to my desires and gifts.

This evaluation, however, must be balanced with the demands of our circumstances. We don't always enjoy a perfect match between who we are and where we minister. God sometimes calls us to places that need our gifts but don't yet realize it, and thus we offer ministries that aren't fully received or appreciated.

So we make adjustments: one pastor attends more committee meetings than she likes because she also gets to preach; another, to maintain church peace, never misses a women's association meeting, though there may be a hundred other things he feels more suited to doing; another still drives a school bus to help make ends meet because he feels called to a rural congregation.

Still, if too many compromises must be made, if there is too great a conflict between gifts and congregational needs, a change may be necessary. Normally, though, a sense of God's will usually emerges in the intersection between who I am and where I am.

Keeping Your Eyes on the Distant Star

Peter Drucker says efficiency is *doing* the thing right, but effectiveness is doing the *right* thing. Effective pastors do the right thing by obeying God's call. But this differs, in most instances, from the pressing thing. The "tyranny of the urgent" always distracts from the most important; shooting at rabbits only scares away the stag. So today must be planned so that we move closer to achieving God's will for us.

Investing time in things that matter, therefore, requires that we keep the vision. Yehudi Menuhin, the great violinist, said, "To play great music you must keep your eyes on a distant star." Accomplishing a great work for Christ requires a similar focus: eyes must be lifted above a thousand and one distractions to the shining goal of what God wants us to do. Otherwise the constant pounding of pressing demands shatters ministry into unrelated bits and pieces of well-meaning ineffectiveness.

In the fall of 1940, the German Luftwaffe rained terror on the city of London, sending an average of 200 planes per raid for fifty-seven consecutive nights. During the days, Winston Churchill, dressed in suit and derby and champing his ever-present cigar, could be seen picking his way through the devastation, encouraging the Londoners he met.

Victory eventually came for Great Britain, of course, and when it did, Churchill was asked what he had done during the interminable nights of the London bombing. He said he had gone to his bomb shelter below Piccadilly Circus and there, with a desk lamp illuminating a map of Europe, had planned the invasion of Germany. Even in the midst of chaos, with victory only a distant star in the dark night, he never lost sight of the vision.

As I consider what God has called me to do, I realize I cannot grow spiritually without certain devotional disciplines. So I begin each day with prayer (along with a mug of coffee!), and because I want to get through the Bible at least once a year, I read two chapters in the Old Testament and two in the New. I must do these things each day if I'm going to fulfill my vision of a growing relationship with God. In a similar way I plan each week (well, most weeks) to set aside time for my family and friends, and even some time for myself.

Likewise, I order my ministry. A few years ago I had one of

those "Aha!" experiences that can dramatically influence one's life. I was reading Peter Drucker's book, *The Effective Executive,* and came across this: "The effective executive focuses on contribution. He looks up from his work and outward toward goals. He asks: 'What can I contribute that will significantly affect the performance and the results of the institution I serve?' "

Suddenly the lights went on for me. I realized I have things to contribute to the church that no one else has, and if I don't contribute what I'm called to contribute, no one else is likely to. Given these facts, I asked myself, *What can I contribute?*

I had to come back to the twin consideration of *who* I am and *where* I am. Soon it became clear that what I could contribute to my church were four things: (1) communicate the gospel as effectively as I'm able through preaching, teaching, and writing; (2) develop an effective leadership team; (3) articulate a vision for the congregation; (4) create an open, positive atmosphere in which a diverse community can flourish.

With these goals in mind, I plan my activities for each week. I set aside time for study in order to have something worthwhile to communicate (for goal one). I meet with the members of my staff and discuss issues with key elders (for goal two). I plan to repeat certain themes in sermons and committee meetings and private conversations (for goals three and four).

I try not to get distracted from these goals. Because I do not feel called to do much pastoral care, I do little counseling and visitation. I'm blessed with others on staff who do these things and do them better than I. But I do some pastoral care, at least in part to fulfill my first goal, because communicators of the gospel must stay in touch with people's needs.

Abraham Lincoln was our greatest President. He kept our nation together through its worst crisis. This was a remarkable feat of leadership. Any modern leader — pastors included — would do well to study carefully his life.

One characteristic of Lincoln was his ability to hold tenaciously the long-range goal of keeping the Union together; he never became distracted from this vision. Everything — no matter how significant — had to be subordinated to the primary goal of pre-serving the Union.

Even slavery. As much as he opposed the institution of hu-man bondage, Lincoln delayed freeing the slaves in order to retain the loyalty of the slave states that supported the Union cause, Mis-souri, Kentucky, and Maryland especially. As a result, Lincoln in-curred the fierce wrath of the northern abolitionists.

Still, in a letter to Horace Greeley, he wrote, "My paramount object in this struggle is to save the Union. . . . If I could save the Union without freeing *any* slave, I would do it, and if I could save it by freeing *all* the slaves, I would do it, and if I could save it by freeing some and leaving others alone I would also do that. . . . I have here stated my purpose according to my view of official duty: and I intend no modification of my oft-expressed personal wish that all men everywhere could be free."

This stance opened Lincoln to criticism from both sides, but he knew his calling and subordinated everything to that goal.

Staying with the Band

Lincoln would not budge from his goal of keeping the Union together, but was open to changing his ideas about how that ought to be achieved. He once signed an order, under severe political pressure, to transfer certain regiments from one field of battle to another. But Secretary of War Edwin M. Stanton refused to carry it out.

"Lincoln is a damn fool for ever signing the order," Stanton snorted.

The remark was passed on to Lincoln, who responded, "If Stanton said I'm a damn fool, then I must be one. He is nearly always right in military matters. I'll step over and find out what his reasoning is."

In contrast, Albert Speer, the brilliant architect of Hitler's wretched Reich, said in his memoirs that he failed because once he made a commitment to Hitler, he never let himself look twice at that commitment. He never examined it, never questioned it.

Wise pastors will occasionally take a second look at their visions, review their goals. I recently became convinced that our church ought to help establish a new church development not far from us. The presbytery, our local denominational governing body, was behind it, and we had the resources and people to make it happen. I discussed it several times with my pastoral staff, but each time the response was underwhelming.

Not easily deflected in my desires, I pressed on, taking the issue to the session, the governing board of the church. I presented the idea, using my best rhetorical gifts and reasoning powers; I sought to convince minds and touch hearts. The response was as animated as a brick wall. The elders expressed no actual opposition but a blankness — nothing.

About three o'clock the next morning, after restless hours of turning my bed sheets into a chaotic mess, I realized what had happened: the leaders were on overload, unable to add another project to an already long list of worthy endeavors. We had just taken the first steps toward establishing an Hispanic congregation; we had recently decided to submit an offer on an adjacent piece of property. Their minds were too full to concentrate on anything else for the time being. I needed to give up. If you're going to lead the parade, you have to stay with the band.

Overcoming Indiscipline

Some days I feel like a pinball bounced from one problem to the next. I assume God is in control (I *am* a Calvinist!), but sometimes I wonder: I'm tossed around by telephone callers, people who stop by, upset staff members, and elders with bright ideas that won't wait. It's tempting to go with the flow, to let myself be carried along by the current of urgent demands. The phrase *organized pastor* sounds like an oxymoron, only a wistful hope at best.

But severe disorganization, like an out-of-control disease, can kill effective ministry. Wherever it rears its frenzied head, we usually find lack of discipline, the failure to take control of our lives and to use time responsibly.

This particular form of sloth, and it often results from a cowardice that reveals itself in an unwillingness to say no, a fear of being unpopular, and a constant flight from discomfort. Discipline demands standing firm, taking the risk of being misunderstood, and staying at something, despite boredom and pain, until it is finished.

William Barclay said that Samuel Taylor Coleridge "is the supreme tragedy of indiscipline. Never did so great a mind produce so little. He left Cambridge University to join the army; he left the army because he could not rub down a horse; he returned to Oxford and left without a degree. He began a paper called *The Watchman* which lived for ten issues and then died. It has been said of him: 'He lost himself in visions of work to be done, that always remained to be done. Coleridge had every poetic gift but one — the gift of sustained and concentrated effort.' In his head and in his mind he had all kinds of books. . . . But the books were never composed outside Coleridge's mind, because he would not face the discipline of sitting down to write them out. No one ever reached any eminence, and no one having reached it ever maintained it, without discipline."

Seizing Our Calendars

How can we cultivate the discipline of organization? By seizing our calendars.

One day it occurred to me: even though many, many people have ideas about how I ought to use my time, I alone bear responsibility for it. One day I will stand before the Judge, and I will not be able to plea, "Well, she said I should. . . . And he told me to. . . ." No, *I* will answer for my stewardship of time. When this dawned on me, I determined to be as thoughtful and as disciplined as possible in my daily schedule.

1. Plan week-long segments. The cycle of seven days is not only a biblical pattern, it is a practical reality for most pastors. We tend to live from Sunday to Sunday (from Judgment Day to Judgment Day!), with a number of consequent deadlines between. It makes sense, therefore, to think in week-long segments.

There are several good organizers on the market. For many years I have used the Daytimer system. In my binder I keep a year's worth of month-at-a-glance pages for noting upcoming events. At the beginning of each month, I insert the day-at-a-glance pages for that month. (In addition to these calendars, I also keep in my binder sermon notes, records of honoraria received, lists of elders and deacons, making it an all-purpose workbook. If I ever lost it, I'd be in a deep pile of trouble!)

On Friday I review the upcoming week, writing in each day's activities on the day-at-a-glance pages. I consider my long-range goals, and I block in activities that will help me reach them, trying to be detailed about the things I intend to do each day (e.g., instead of writing "Study," I write, "Read 20 pages of Barth, *CD — IV/1*, and get caught up on back issues of *Christianity Today*). At the bottom of each day's page, I list telephone calls that need to be made.

In general, I do administration at the beginning of my week and study and sermon preparation at the end. On Mondays I write correspondence (rarely, if ever, have I had mail that couldn't wait until the next Monday for a reply), and I spend a good deal of time on the telephone (talking with committee chairpersons, recruiting, lighting fires under slow movers, and putting out the fires of the agitated).

Tuesday mornings are set aside for exegeting my upcoming sermon text, and the afternoon is devoted to staff meetings and preparing the order of worship. I try to keep Wednesday flexible, often writing for publication or preparing for teaching. By Thursday I'm working on my sermon, giving much of the day to brainstorming and outlining. On Friday mornings I write my sermon; all telephone calls are held, and staff members know they dare not interrupt except for *serious* emergencies. I clean off my desk that afternoon and make sure the following week is planned.

Throughout the week, I schedule periodic counseling appointments, usually in late afternoons, which not only reserves my mornings for study but also seems to be most convenient for people who work.

2. *Do first things first.* Andrew Carnegie was once hired as a management consultant. He said, "I'll make one suggestion, and you send me a check for what you think it's worth. Write down what you have to do on a piece of paper in order of priority, and complete the first item before you go to the second." The business-

man to whom he offered this advice eventually sent him a check for $10,000.

In the words of Peter Drucker, "Effective executives do first things first, and they do one thing at a time. . . . There was Mozart, of course. He could, it seems, work on several compositions at the same time, all of them masterpieces. But he is the only known exception. The other prolific composers of the first rank — Bach, for instance, Handel, or Haydn, or Verdi — composed one work at a time. They did not begin the next until they had finished the preceding one, or until they had stopped work on it for the time being and put it away in the drawer. Executives can hardly assume that they are 'executive Mozarts.' "

This sounds so simple, so obvious. But when the first thing on your list is to call an elder angry about last Sunday's sermon or confront a staff member who has been letting things fall through the cracks or form an outline for a text that seems dull — well, doing first things first isn't easy. Procrastination comes to the rescue with all sorts of excuses; boredom cries out for relief; other things suddenly become much more urgent.

I've noticed how much needs my attention Friday mornings when I should be writing my sermon: my pencils need sharpening (*all* of them), my desk drawers need cleaning, my plastic plant needs watering. Eventually, though, as the morning starts slipping away, I must force myself to do what needs to be done whether I feel like it or not.

Actually, a comfort comes in focusing on one thing at a time. If we always have our eyes set on the distant horizon, we'll despair of making any progress. When we see nothing but the vision of doubling the size of our church or building a great staff or writing a book, we can easily end each day overwhelmed with all we didn't accomplish, with all the distance still left to travel.

Well-known commentator Eric Sevareid said that the best lesson he ever learned was the principle of the next mile: "During World War II, I and several others had to parachute from a crippled Army transport plane into mountainous jungle on the Burma/India border. It was several weeks before an armed relief expedition could reach us, and then we began a painful, plodding march out to civilized India. We were faced with a 140-mile trek, over mountains in August heat and monsoon rains. In the first hour of the march I rammed a boot nail deep into one foot; by evening I had bleeding blisters the size of fifty-cent pieces on both feet. Could I hobble 140 miles? Could the others, some in worse shape than I, complete such a distance? We were convinced we could not. But we *could* hobble to that ridge, we *could* make the next friendly village for the night. And that, of course, was all we had to do. . . ."

3. *Plan for interruptions.* At the end of a tiring day, I sometimes comment to my family, "If it weren't for people, ministry would be a breeze!" But ministry involves people, and people guarantee interruptions. Along with death and taxes, interruptions are a certainty, no matter how forcefully the calendar is seized, no matter how many secretaries stand guard.

Two things have helped me cope with this. First, in my study of the Gospels, I discovered how much of Jesus' ministry happened because of interruptions. His miracles and teaching often took place in response to unscheduled pleas for help and questions. He couldn't even take a vacation without finding a crowd waiting for him when he arrived! I began to realize that if Jesus did kingdom business this way, I needed to get used to interruptions. If the Lord himself wasn't too important to be sidetracked by the unexpected, who was I to resent it?

So do we just give up and let ourselves be dominated by the loudest voices and most demanding people? No, we keep trying to be good stewards of our calendars, but we expect the inevitable.

The second thing that helped me deal with intrusions in my day was learning how to schedule them on my calendar. I know they will happen, I expect good things in ministry to result from them, and so I now make room for them. I try never to plan a day too tightly; I keep my to-do list manageable enough so that when Mrs. Smith calls and "really must" see me, well, she can.

4. *Never accept new responsibilities without prayer and reflection.* Refusing a request for time can be difficult for at least two reasons: it feels good to be wanted, and it feels bad to disappoint others. For me, this has too often meant saying yes to things for which I had neither time nor inclination. Then, as pressures mounted, a slight

bitterness would seep into my ministry — not much, but enough to foul the sweet joy of service.

In recent years I have adopted a rule: I never say yes or no at the time I'm asked to do something. I take at least twenty-four hours to pray and think about it. I generally say something like, "So far as I can see, my calendar looks clear, but I want to pray about it. I want to make sure this would be a good use of my gifts. I will call you in a day or two to inform you of my decision."

During this time of prayer and reflection, I ask myself several questions: Is this something for which I have gifts? Does this fit the vision for ministry God has given me? Am I being unduly influenced by the honor of being asked or the prestige of the occasion? Would saying yes to this mean saying no to something more important?

Gordon MacDonald makes a helpful distinction between the *driven* and the *called*. Driven people strive to do as much as possible, and they often accomplish a great deal, though at significant cost to themselves and others. Called people, on the other hand, do what the Father sets before them.

From God's call comes perseverance. A sense of call enabled Raymond Lull, the first missionary to the Arabs, to labor his entire lifetime with only one convert. A driven man would have demanded more results, more "success."

And from God's call comes peace. John Donne prayed, "Keep us, Lord, so awake in the duties of our callings that we may sleep in your peace and wake in your glory." Staying at the duties of our callings, and not taking on the burden of saving the world, keeps us in the peace that passes all understanding.

Finding time for things that matter, then, means first and foremost discovering God's call, and his peace.

When my congregation grants me freedom to minister outside our church, they are giving me, my gifts, and even some of themselves to others.

— *Maxie Dunnam*

CHAPTER TEN
Ministry Outside the Congregation

Y ou receive a phone call one afternoon: "Pastor, a group of us in the community have become increasingly troubled about child abuse. A number of leaders in the religious and social service communities are gathering this Thursday night to see what we can do to help. Your colleague at Good Shepherd Lutheran Church suggested you might want to join us. Do you think you can?"

You pause, not knowing what to say, although you're already feeling guilty. In milliseconds a number of concerns cross your mind: *Is this a problem I'm qualified to tackle? Do I have the time? My preaching has been suffering, and I've already decided to spend more time on it. But I'd hate to say no to such a genuine need. Besides, wouldn't this be a great opportunity to represent the church in the community? There may be some evangelistic opportunities, as well. Then again, my schedule is loaded.*

You finally tell the caller that you'll be happy to come to the organizing meeting, but you're not sure what you'll be able to do after that. You realize, however, that you've just postponed your decision and that your questions have yet to be resolved.

Pastors are regularly presented with opportunities for ministry outside their congregations, certainly more opportunities than they can say yes to: parachurch board membership, denominational committee work, writing and speaking opportunities — the list goes on.

Sometimes ministry outside the congregation seems like a distraction; at other times it feels like a blessing. In deciding whether and how to take such opportunities, here are some things I keep in mind.

The Value of Outside Ministry

When a pastor ministers outside the congregation, the church loses his or her time and availability. The person who substitutes in the pulpit may be less effective. An emergency may not receive immediate attention. But in my mind, these drawbacks are outweighed by five benefits.

1. It helps the local church. Especially in a growing and thriving church, we can become so wrapped up in keeping the church out of chaos that we may miss influences, ideas, and streams of ministry that can positively feed our ministries. Outside ministries can give us insights that can help our congregation for years to come.

One pastor friend says that he was reluctant to participate in a local suicide prevention committee. It seemed like a problem that was beyond his skills or background. But he did learn a great deal about what leads people to suicide, and that helped him be much more sensitive to emotionally troubled members in his congregation.

A church is like a pond. It remains fresh and full when water flows in and out; without that, it grows stagnant or dries up.

2. *It broadens my circle of relationships.* For several years I have served on the local board of the Metropolitan Interfaith Association, an ecumenical social services agency in Memphis, where I have become acquainted with individuals I would not have met otherwise. One pastor I met there has become one of my best friends in Memphis. I have preached for him on several occasions, and his friendship has enriched my life in many ways.

3. *It helps the community.* Many needs in a community cannot be met by one church alone but only as churches cooperate. Through outside ministry, pastors build the network of relationships that contribute to church teamwork and can impact the community significantly.

Several years ago a professor at Mid-America Seminary in Memphis organized quarterly prayer breakfasts for the pastors of the larger evangelical churches.

Those meetings accomplished several things. I got to know each pastor personally, discovering his or her personality, ministry style, vision, and background. Also, the meetings diminished competition between our churches. When our members knew we were meeting with each other and building relationships, it fostered trust and unity among the churches.

These relationships have been the entrée for working together. When the city experienced tension concerning our new black mayor, the relationships were sufficiently established for me to suggest we publish an open letter in the local newspaper calling for support of the new mayor.

4. *It opens doors for members' community involvement.* Many people want to serve their community but don't know how or where. If their pastor works in a community ministry, it gives not only confidence in the ministry but a willingness to get involved.

Several years ago I became interested in the work of Marva Collins. She organized and leads a school for at-risk children, primarily African-American children in the inner city of Chicago. Her approach is unique, with an integrated curriculum that emphasizes practical skills as well as the study of great literature, problem solving, and phonics. After she spoke in Memphis, my concern for inner city children grew. I decided to put together a community group to form an explicitly Christian school, which we've called Shepherd School, based on the Collins model. Our goal is to set up a number of small schools throughout the community.

Even though Shepherd School is not a ministry of our church, and even though it is a risky idea, many of our people have already shown interest in helping with the work. I think my involvement is a key reason for that interest.

5. It gives our church a larger forum. For over five years I have served as chairperson for the evangelism committee of the World Methodist Council. I see this not just as my ministry but as an extension of our church's ministry. I am the church's mouthpiece, enabling the church to speak and reach beyond its locale.

I believe the local church needs a corporate witness, someone representing what it preaches in the community each week, bringing the name of the church into the community and modeling its message. If the pastor is preaching about the need to help the poor and feed the hungry, the church needs an official representative in the community doing that.

How to Choose Involvements

As I mentioned, the average pastor receives numerous requests to become involved in outside ministries. We can't take them all. How do we decide which to join? I ask myself some of the following questions.

• *Will it help the community?* My first concern is whether the endeavor will be effective at helping people in need.

For example, our church is committed to the poor in Memphis. I want to do anything I can to solve housing, educational, nutrition, and employment problems in Memphis. That has been the basis for our decision to support the Shepherd School and our annual building of a house in the Habitat for Humanity program.

I'm currently involved in an ad hoc committee putting together a city-wide, ecumenical, evangelism campaign in Memphis. I'm taking time for this because city-wide events have a spiritual impact, reach, and visibility that local churches can't have.

• *Will it pay off for me personally?* A limited number of ministries benefit the pastor himself. Most pastors feel obligated to attend the local ministerial association, but that doesn't have enough pay-off for me. I do involve myself in other networks of clergy, however.

Especially early in our careers, we need to be careful to build habits of involvement that give a good return. I know one young pastor who would go to the hospital in the county seat and visit every Methodist patient. I felt early on I could better use my time visiting only the most critical patients and using the rest for reading or preparing messages or community work.

Some outside ministries may not be necessary, but they are tremendously rewarding. They keep me alive, fresh, and growing. Leonard Sweet, president of United Theological Seminary, in Dayton, Ohio, has put together an ecumenical group for a three-year project: to develop an apologetic for the twenty-first century.

That interested me, so I accepted his invitation. I want to move into that intellectual world and be sensitized to its ideas. Far from draining me, that type of project fuels me. Whatever level of interaction we have and whatever type of interest, there are ways to plug in somewhere and contribute to a more vital self.

• *Will it pay off for our church?* If I'm going to take time away from the church, I want the church to benefit somehow, directly or indirectly.

Our church has made a decision to make ministry to the recovering community — those trying to come out of life-destroying habits — a priority. First, the recovering community is large and needy. Second, since our church is investing significant time, energy, and money, we know that some recovering people will make our church their own — a side benefit we have no inclination to ignore!

The other side of this question is, *Will my involvement hurt the church?* Periodically I track how many hours I give to the church and to outside ministry. I would not feel comfortable with spending more than 20 percent of my time on outside ministry. No matter my hours, if significant church needs are untended, that's a sign I need to cut back. To a large extent our own efficiency and effectiveness determines how many hours we can spend away.

● *Will it fairly represent my church?* It is impossible for you to be involved in the public arena and not have your church associated with your actions. You can't divorce yourself from your congregation. For that reason, I don't feel free to become involved in partisan politics: I don't endorse candidates nor work for their election. Furthermore, my church would not smile on my marching in a public demonstration unless it was a clear moral issue.

● *Will it overly drain me?* While some outside ministry is stimulating, other obligations sap my energy. Denominational committees and administrative roles generally take the life out of me. I fulfill some obligations like that out of a sense of responsibility, but others I turn down without any sense of guilt. I've found they take too much out of me.

Convincing the Congregation

If for some reason I've been out of the pulpit several weeks in a row, speaking at conferences or other churches, members will kid me: "If you take many more trips, we're going to introduce you as the guest speaker instead of the pastor." We all laugh about that, but I know the kidding is based on some level of concern.

Congregations have a right to expect the bulk of their pastors' attention. What people sometimes forget, though, is that in limited quantities, outside involvement actually benefits them.

So, the more we explain the benefits of outside ministry to our congregation, the more willing they will be to free us for that purpose, and just as important, the more support they will give us. Here's how I encourage their support.

● *Be effective at the home base.* Getting the job done at home frees me to minister elsewhere without having a general uprising. If administrative details are in disarray, if we lack teachers for the classroom, if weekly church services are sloppy, my people will rightly question the wisdom of my commitment elsewhere. Especially if outside ministry calls me from the pulpit on Sunday, I'd better be paying my dues.

One pastor I know in the Northwest became interested in the problem of racism, researched the subject heavily, and became heavily involved as an activist for equal rights, to the point where he virtually abandoned his congregation. Because of this neglect, his church eventually asked him to resign his church responsibilities.

Effectiveness at home does more than quell uprisings, though. It legitimizes our outside work. Rather than being an individual working in the community, I represent a group of concerned people. It also makes resources available for the outside involvement. People from my church often volunteer as workers, and money is often budgeted in support of such programs.

● *Come to an agreement with your congregation and communicate that clearly.* Many of my people have not been supportive of my participation in the World Methodist Council because they haven't thought the Council supports their values and beliefs.

But these same people are enthused about my work with The Methodist Declaration, an ad hoc group seeking to keep the Methodist Church centered in traditional orthodoxy. The issues addressed by this ad hoc group have been on the minds of many of our church members, and they were delighted for me to voice their convictions in this group.

In general, then, I've found that churches support their pastor's outside ministry if it is (a) an extension of the church's personality, and (b) in accord with their idea of ministry. Not all my outside involvement has to meet these criteria, but most better.

Thus, I've seen the need to become more formal in the way I become involved in outside ministries. Our staff/parish committee reviewed my involvement in outside ministry recently, set a new policy, and clearly communicated that with the congregation. We've agreed to see my ministry as majoring in three areas:

— The local church: preaching, casting vision, planning, and legitimizing ministry.

— The community of Memphis: primarily, the recovering community and the poor.

— The denomination.

Previously the church's policy was that I could be absent from the pulpit eight Sundays a year (including my vacation time). After this recent review, that was bumped to ten Sundays. This agreement was approved by the board and communicated to the congregation in writing.

● *Let the congregation see the value of what I'm doing.* I intentionally weave my outside ministry experiences into my sermons as anecdotes. As people see the spiritual impact of my time away, based on my conversations and experiences, they feel included in what I do, they see God at work, and they catch my vision.

Along with four other large churches in our denomination, our church is helping some Russian churches with evangelism. Recently I visited Russia to make contacts and determine what help we could give. The first Sunday after my return, I did more than tell a few anecdotes; I preached a sermon entitled "From Russia with Love." In that sermon I told this story:

We spent time in Russia with one church that helps feed hungry, elderly, starving pensioners. One day we helped the volunteers serve food. It was an amazing thing — many of those hungry people, 60, 70, 80 years old, have never been served in their lives. What expressions would come on their faces when we would approach them and shake their hands!

I helped two people to a table and then gave them trays of food. They each received a bowl of rice, a bowl of hot soup, a piece of bread, a piece of meat, and a cup of hot tea. Then I sat down beside one woman.

I learned through an interpreter that the woman was 76 years old. Her face lit up as she told me that she had a Ph.D. in geology and had served the government in Siberia for thirty-five years. Then her face clouded, and she said, "But the dream is dead. The dream is gone."

Her pension of five hundred rubles had been adequate for years, but no longer. She can't buy a dress, much less a coat. She felt betrayed. She was without hope. Her soul has been sucked out.

Such firsthand experiences animate sermons and inform our

church of great needs in the world. The value of my time away from the church is obvious to all.

I still struggle how to make best use of my time as a pastor. But these guidelines take away a lot of the anguish, and they free me to serve better my congregation and the larger human community to which Christ calls me.

Mere change energizes me, even when the change means demanding work.

— *Maxie Dunnam*

CHAPTER ELEVEN

When It's Time to Get Away

I was scheduled to get away from the church for two weeks — study leave and vacation. But I was a little uncomfortable as I got in my car.

As usual, I was leaving with a few ends not neatly tied up: some committees were in the middle of making important decisions, some people needed visiting in the hospital, and I wasn't sure how well the guest preachers I had lined up would be received.

On top of that, some people were not particularly happy with me — not a good situation for a pastor who had been at the church only about a year.

One of our part-time staff members was discovered to have cancer, and we had held a prayer service for her healing. Since healing services were something new to our church, some members, who were already questioning how Methodist their new minister was, saw this as the final straw.

Even though I felt unsettled, I was determined to get away. I rationalized to myself, *Everything will take care of itself.*

It's tough to get away from the church for vacation, study leave, or retreats. Many pastors feel a twinge of guilt leaving: *Is this really going to be best for the church?* Many members feel the church runs on three cylinders while we're gone. And if there's any trouble brewing, we're not sure what we'll come back to.

Still we know, from experience and from the advice of others, that getting away is absolutely vital. How to do it smoothly, with a minimum of disruption to the church, and productively, with a maximum of refreshment for me, is the question. Here are a few things I've discovered.

Periodic Pep Talks

When we're feeling the pressure of daily ministry, we're not inclined to plan a getaway. Or if we have planned one, as the time approaches, we begin wondering if it's an appropriate time to take off. We just can't imagine how the church can get along without us for two weeks!

Put that way it sounds silly, but when we're in that frame of mind, it seems to make sense. The best antidote to such thinking is to remind myself periodically of what getting away does for me and the congregation.

1. It renews my energy. Most of us get the physical rest we need; what we lack is emotional and mental rest. Just as farm fields are maximized by rotating crops, so a change can refresh us. Winston Churchill said that a change is as good as a rest. I've found that to be true for me.

Change energizes me even when the change is demanding

work. When I write for publication, for instance, the work is often painstaking, but it refreshes me. The interlude away from people and the intellectual challenge provide emotional refuge. I'm able to turn my mind away from weighty church problems, and it's not long before I feel lighter.

2. *I see the big picture again.* The obligations and demands of people in need, an organization to be led, and the weekly sermon to be created consume great amounts of energy. If I do not disengage, I soon begin to narrow my sights to what's around the next bend. I forget the long-range goal of the journey I'm on.

Times away, though, return my long-range vision. My study retreats, in which I plan out my sermons for six months to a year, strengthen me immensely even though they are hard work. Just seeing what I'll be preaching in the coming months makes me enthusiastic for the future.

3. *I grow in my pastoral skills and confidence.* One pastor I know was struggling with his preaching. His personnel committee had told him some months earlier to give his preaching more attention. He'd been reading and reflecting for months, but he wasn't sure he was making progress.

He decided to take a seminar in preaching. As part of the course, he was to write and present the first few minutes of a sermon. One seminar leader, one of the premier preaching professors in the nation, told him, "I can tell you're a good preacher." The pastor was elated. He knew he would never become superb, but he got the outside affirmation he needed to regain his confidence.

I take two, two-week study leaves each year. My people are always excited and affirming when I return. They can tell the difference it makes in my preaching.

4. *My passion for ministry is renewed.* One youth pastor I know found himself becoming increasingly discouraged with his ministry. He couldn't point to anything specific, but he didn't seem to be enjoying it any longer.

When he told this to a group of colleagues he met with regularly, the first question they asked was, "Have you taken a day off lately?"

"Well, sort of," he replied.

"What do you mean 'Sort of'?"

"Well, I usually get part of Monday to play golf."

"But have you gotten any sustained break from ministry, for a minimum of 24 hours?" they pestered.

He said he hadn't, and they gently scolded him to do so.

Soon afterward, he found an old, beat-up, ten-speed bike at a garage sale. He put ministry on hold for about a week as he dismantled, sanded, and painted the frame, repacked the bearings and oiled the gears.

To this young man's surprise, he found his passion to fix a bike had fixed his lack of passion for ministry. Once again he was excited about his work with youth.

A deliberate break, even a short one, relieves us from the dullness-producing pressure of a demanding routine.

5. *The congregation appreciates me more.* The old adage is true: absence makes the heart grow fonder. Church members are happy for a break as well. They enjoy hearing another preacher or two: it's a new voice, with new inflection, and fresh illustrations! But the guests are not their pastor. And even though they happily live without him or her for a few weeks, that's the pastor they want back.

Break Signals

Given the nature of our work, we can't wait until we're exhausted and then just take off. Besides, I've found that physical fatigue isn't the only signal that I need an oasis. Still, we need to monitor our rhythms so that we can better plan our vacations and retreats. Here are signs that tell me I'm not getting enough time away.

• *Relational dullness.* I fail to pick up on people's emotions and relational signals. I lose my sensitivity to what people need and expect of me. I notice it first with my wife and then with staff.

Recently my wife asked when I had last seen Dr. Long, my

ear-nose-and-throat specialist. My throat flares up now and then, especially when I'm under unusual stress and have a heavy speaking schedule. I assumed she was concerned about my throat.

When I told her I had been in to see him recently, she immediately asked, "Did he check your hearing?" She had spoken to me several times that night, and I had not responded. She was naturally concerned.

The problem was not my hearing, however, but my dulled sensitivities. Times like these are sure signs that I need a change of pace.

• *Mental sluggishness.* My thoughts come slowly; I'm not creative; I lack enthusiasm for even my favorite activities. I even find it difficult to participate in normal conversation.

This year we inaugurated a new leadership/management style in our church. Our administrative board is the ruling body of the church and numbers 155, but since we had found that group too cumbersome, we instituted a new working group of fifteen, an executive committee.

At the first meeting I was sluggish in sharing the vision. The meeting lacked life and direction. I thought, *Boy, we may have made a big mistake in instituting this new style of administration.*

The second meeting, however, was a joy. The people were excited. We made three big decisions. There was a sense of spiritual discernment and openness.

I reflected later on the difference. I had been worn-out at the first meeting. I had come through our General Conference (regional denominational meeting) which had been a pressure-cooker. I had been mentally and physically exhausted. Before the second meeting, I had had a few days off, had gone to three movies in a week, and was fresh in mind and body.

Overcoming the Difficulties

Getting away is never easy. The pulpit needs to be filled. Emergencies that need the pastor arise. Decisions must be delayed. Staff and volunteers must shoulder extra work. Here's how I deal with these inevitable difficulties.

• *Manage the guilt.* The book title *When I Relax, I Feel Guilty* expresses the feelings of many pastors. Most pastors with strong work ethics can't help but feel guilty stepping out the door. It may be neurotic guilt, but it's there nonetheless.

Generally, I've learned to dissipate this type of guilt by simply reminding myself of the hours I've been putting in as well as the Lord's permission, nay *command*, to take periodic rest.

But I still feel guilty when my schedule gets so contorted that I'm out of the pulpit for three or more Sundays in a row. That's when it's most inconvenient for the church. And lay leaders rightly worry about visitors who come and don't get to hear me preach.

This past summer I was away for five straight weeks, and that's just too long. But there was nothing I could do about it. All I could do was make a note to myself to be especially watchful to minimize consecutive Sundays out of the pulpit.

• *Handle the serious emergencies.* Most emergencies (illnesses, operations, deaths) can be handled by other staff members or clergy from nearby churches. But I've always had a special concern about being out of town when a longstanding member becomes gravely ill or dies. I've finally decided that, if at all possible, I'll return for the funeral.

Sometimes that requires a little creativity. Recently I was teaching at a seminar in Florida when the Bible teacher in our day school, around whom the day school revolved, died after a long battle with cancer. I was torn about what to do, but it turned out that I was able to shift my final presentation so that I could conduct this woman's funeral.

• *Expect to do double duty before and after.* Especially in a smaller church, where the pastor is the hub of the wheel, everything from getting the front door unlocked on Sunday morning to making sure the mortgage gets paid can be a vital concern while the pastor's away.

Hard work before leaving and when I return is the only way to prevent problems and slip ups. That means I line up guest preachers; I make sure someone oversees the Sunday morning worship routines; I line up staff or colleagues from other churches to make hospital calls, if necessary; I check with committee chairpersons about any input they need from me; I temporarily cancel some activities that absolutely need my presence; I brief my secretary on correspondence that needs to be taken care of without me; and on it goes. It's exhausting just remembering what I have to do.

At times, this doesn't seem fair. It's like I'm paying double for a time away that is part of my contract. But I've come to see that is just the nature of pastoral getaways.

Making the Most of Getaways

While I was pastoring in Southern California, I once drove several hours to a mountain cabin. I was eagerly looking forward to a mini, three-day study leave. As I unpacked the car upon my arrival, I discovered I had forgotten all my resources and study books. I didn't even have a Bible!

Fuming inside, I debated whether to make the four-hour round trip for the books. Finally I decided to stay and simply rest, reflect, pray, and meditate. That trip turned out to be one of the most creative times in my entire life.

The fact that I didn't have books forced me to pursue another agenda, and that turned out to be what I needed more than anything. It was the first time I had experienced a retreat of solitude and prayer. With nothing to read, I could only reflect, pray, be silent, and write. This was such a spiritually renewing experience that ever since, I have regularly taken similar 24- to 48-hour renewal retreats.

That experience serendipitously taught me that as important as it is to have a plan of attack when I get away, I can gain a great deal if I remain open to whatever the experience hands me.

That being said, I still feel that planning well each type of getaway tends to ensure greater success. Here are some of the types of getaways I take and how I arrange them to benefit me the most.

• *Study retreats.* I've never taken a sabbatical and don't feel the need for one. I think that's because of the way I arrange study leaves each year.

I schedule two, two-week study periods each year (one Sunday is missed each time), one around Labor Day weekend and the other usually just before Lent. My study retreats are dedicated solely to researching and preparing sermons. I take three or four boxes of books and files, and for fifteen hours a day I read, outline, and write messages.

My schedule on these retreats is flexible, to make the most of my energies and concentration. Some nights, if I'm on a roll, I'll study until three in the morning and then sleep in. Other nights I'll eat a nice dinner, take a long walk, go to bed, and then hit the books at six in the morning. I often take long walks as breaks.

Usually I hole up in a condominium where I know I'll be isolated. Sometimes my wife accompanies me, but if so, she has her own projects.

I don't do any general reading during study leaves. All my time and energies are focused on the sermons for the months ahead. In my normal schedule, I keep books and magazines nearby and read snatches hear and there.

● *Spiritual renewal.* As I mentioned above, I now schedule a time for concentrated spiritual reflection every three to four months. For me a spiritual renewal is a day or two in which I attempt to rest physically while focusing my attention spiritually.

Most of my time is spent assessing myself: what's going on in my family and my life, how I feel about my ministry. I think about what directions I need to be going and decisions I need to make. Such reflection is part of my nightly routine, but these little retreats give me a chance to go much deeper.

For my spiritual retreats to be effective, I've found it essential to get away from the house. My study is at home, equipped with a phone, of course. If I stay home, I invariably end up at my desk working on a sermon or some writing project, or I will be interrupted by a call. I need isolation; I need to cocoon so that later I can fly.

Recently I was asked to consider another ministry position. I wrestled with the decision for months but couldn't get a clear direction. Two weeks before I was to respond, I took off for a prayer retreat, alone. I did not see another person for 48 hours.

During that time I felt a clear direction from the Spirit that I was not to make the move. Without that retreat, I'm not sure I would have had the discernment needed.

• *Days off.* Thursday is my set day off, but I take that perhaps once a month. Instead, on Saturday mornings I try to finish up last-minute preparations for the Sunday service, reviewing the liturgy, Scripture readings, and hymns — no sermon preparation, though — and then relax for the rest of the day. So, weekly I take about three-fourths of a day off. In addition, every six weeks or so I will take a two-day trip to see my parents.

Having an enjoyable activity — Churchill's change that refreshes — is important for my time off. In California, my hobby was sailing. Lately Jerry and I have taken up visiting estate sales and auctions, and I have started collecting art, both for pleasure and investment.

But my rhythms and habits have changed over the years. When my children were living at home, I was more careful to mark out a day to be with the family. When the kids were smaller and we lived in California, I would pick them up from school on Friday, and two times a month we would go to the beach, camping in our little trailer, returning Saturday evening.

• *Family holidays and vacations.* My holidays and vacations revolve around family rituals. Someone said that love is half history and half intuition. When our children (my youngest is now 26) get together to reminisce, more than anything they talk about the rituals.

They remember that when we lived in California, every summer we'd drive cross country back to the South to visit both sets of grandparents. Our children recall how we would stop at one public pool in Arizona so that they could swim.

Each year we also took a "snow vacation," traveling to the mountains two hours north of us to one of our church camps that was not in use at that time. Every Thanksgiving while in California, we spent time with two pastors' families, and we would always have a touch football game on Thursday afternoon. The memories of these rituals have become some of the glue of our family. They've also been some of the fuel that has energized my ministry.

In addition to vacations, I try to take advantage of conferences or special trips. This summer I will be involved in a meeting in Bulgaria, so Jerry, my wife, is coming with me. We'll take a week of vacation after the meeting is over.

In addition to defraying some travel expenses, the initial time spent in a meeting helps to begin the process of disengagement from church obligations, so that when the vacation starts, I can more quickly enjoy myself.

If I've had a good break from ministry, when I return to the church it takes me a while to get back into the routine. But invariably the juices start flowing once I return to the pace of ministry. The shepherd's staff feels comfortable in my hand, it tastes sweet to stand in the pulpit, and I once again relish the call God has placed on my life.

You cannot hold anyone accountable, and you cannot hold yourself accountable for growth, unless in advance you've determined your mission and goals and the criteria to measure them.

— Gordon MacDonald

CHAPTER TWELVE
Investing Your Life Wisely

When I was in college, I participated in a campus ministry whose aim was the evangelization of the whole world. The audacity of the dream ignited new passion within my personal faith, and for that I'm grateful. But sometimes I suspect the motivational approaches went a bit too far.

One day, for example, a staff member read us a story from the biography of C. T. Studd, one of the great English missionary pioneers of the nineteenth century. We'd all come to revere Studd as one who gave up everything — including a great sports career —to evangelize the nations. We listened intently for further insights that would enable us to imitate this man and his faith.

As I recall, Studd went off to Africa and remained there seventeen years without seeing his English homeland. He never saw his wife, either, since she remained in England to assist the supporting mission organization. For reasons I cannot fathom now, we assumed this willingness to accept marital separation was admirable, the epitome of commitment.

Now here's the story we heard that day: Studd's wife eventually came to Africa, but only because it seemed prudent for her — get this — to visit the various mission outposts. So her husband's mission station became part of the itinerary.

As I remember the story, she came up a river by boat to the place where Studd was living. He met her and walked her to the front porch of his house. There they stayed for thirty or so minutes, visiting about the progress of "winning the lost" and then having a time of prayer. Then she returned to her boat and continued her tour.

We students were breathless when we heard this story. "What extraordinary dedication!" we said to one another. "This is what it's all about. If God is to use us, these are the kinds of people we've got to become."

As far as I know, none of us ever became those kinds of people, and that's probably good. I still admire C. T. Studd, but not his perspective on marriage.

Occasionally, I've pondered the wisdom we employ in choosing role models. In this case we simply didn't know the whole story. We selected a "sound bite" out of a good man's life and used it to exemplify sacrifice and dedication. The possibility never occurred to us that C. T. Studd may have had a substandard marriage, or that what Studd and his wife did might have been just plain wrong.

Maybe the fact that he didn't rush to the river — after all, he had been an athlete — and scoop her up in his arms and smother her with kisses (even though we are talking about a Victorian culture) says something that's sad. At age 53 I now know something I didn't know at 19: there's no way I would leave my wife for seventeen years. And if something had necessitated a separation of that period of time, I wouldn't have chosen to spend the thirty minutes sitting on a front porch talking about missions.

The faith tradition in which I was raised was built on the crusader model. It is shaped, first and foremost, by the belief that we have a message of salvation to give to the nations, which must be proclaimed at all costs. It follows, then, that the heroes are those who proclaim that message at whatever sacrifice is necessary. Studd is an example of this apostolic lifestyle: preach the gospel with nothing held back.

Our teachers seldom made clear to us that apostle-types tend to be strange (if wonderful) people. They are not always good husbands or wives, good parents, or specimens of good health. They are often poor at team-building or team-playing. Get too close to them, and you discover that their strengths are awesome — but so are their flaws.

But since we rarely hear about the flaws — and those brave enough to tell us about them have usually found their comments unwelcomed — we conjure up images of superlative people who set the standard.

We grow discouraged when that doesn't happen. We want to be like C. T. Studd, but then we also want to be a good spouse, a good parent, a good team player, a good preacher, a good caregiver, and on and on. It doesn't work, because there is probably no such thing as a well-rounded hero. So more than a few of us live lives of quiet dissatisfaction because we do not measure up to the standards we've set for ourselves.

Today, the heroes may be different: not the missionary pioneer of yesterday but the entrepreneurial leaders who have unusual gifts and build megachurch institutions that attract, evangelize (I think), and mobilize thousands of people. Some of these I am fortunate to call my friends. I admire them; I don't think I envy them.

But I must be candid. I would have twenty years ago. At the age of 30, I would have hungered for that sort of effectiveness. I would have brooded on what it might take to offer such leadership. I would have studied these entrepreneurial leaders as carefully as possible so that I could be like them and experience their success.

If there are virtues to growing older, one of them is to slowly lose the need to be like everyone else — especially the most successful heroes. To gain a bit of maturity is first to see that "the Spirit gives gifts to whom he will," and to see that with all the success and privilege comes significant "bondage." Being a leader is wonderful. But it is not without its price.

There is enormous spiritual pressure in the seduction of pride and competition. There are potential "soft addictions" of sensation, excitement, applause, and being the center of attention. There are the desperately lonely moments when one in the spotlight realizes that there are many acquaintances but few friends and little time for friendships.

For leaders there is the anxiety of wondering what this notoriety is doing to the family, especially the children. The bondage goes on and on.

No, there is little to envy or copy among the heroes. God knows which ones are his, and he knows why they are successful. And most of the time I'm glad it's them and not me.

As I said, there were times when I measured myself against the heroes of the past and the present. Then I realized one day that there were one or two young men measuring themselves against me. I wasn't measuring up to *my* models, and they were upset because they weren't measuring up to me.

This measurement stuff — when the criteria is someone else's achievements or personality — has to be seen for what it is: a sure menu for misery.

My father had been a successful pastor in his younger years, a hero to more than a few in his time. So in the first years of my pastoral life, I measured myself against him. I'd think, *When my father was my age, he was preaching to seven hundred people. I'm preaching to only one hundred. What's wrong with me?*

Later on, I found myself in a congregation several times the size of his largest, and I remember having an empty feeling. I'd exceeded his numbers. Why didn't I feel better about it? And why was I now measuring myself against someone else (always with bigger numbers)?

One day my dad and I were comparing notes about the contrasts between his ministry and mine.

"You guys have to worry about so many programs today," he said. "You are all glorified CEO's. There's not a one of you in these large churches who can honestly call himself a pastor. Pastors care for people; you run programs and build institutions."

"You didn't worry about programs?" I asked.

"Oh, there were a few," he said.

"How many?"

"Basically three," he answered.

"Three?" I was leading a church that had 137 programs (we counted them one time), and he had only three?

"Yeah, three," he said. "I was responsible for Sunday services, calling on people during the week, and leading the prayer service on Wednesday night. I spent my time with the sick, the unsaved, and the men who were trying to build strong families."

"What about Christian education?" I wondered.

"Some of the women took care of that."

"Didn't they bring you their recruitment problems, their circular debates, all their — "

"No, none of that was considered a pastor's responsibility. I told you; I led people to Christ, called on the sick, and every once in a while, had to go out to the local bar and bring a drunk home to his wife and help him sober up."

Maybe my dad was right. The new CEO pastor is a marketer, a manager, a publicist, a systems analyzer, a small-groups mobilizer.

Then again, the pastor is expected to communicate like Campolo, lead like Criswell, think like Packer, and theologize like Stott, be prophetic like Colson, and evangelize like Graham.

Perhaps we've made a dangerous move by sizing up ourselves on the basis of our ability to grow large, impressive organizations. We hear less and less about the quality of a leader's spirit. The conferences — for the most part — are all about the "market," the institution, the program.

Perhaps this is not all bad, except when it is compared with the amount of time on the subject of soul and its capacity to be prophetic, perceptive, and powerful.

Typical Illusions

For two of the years I was in seminary, I pastored a tiny country church 175 miles east of Denver. For a year, Gail and I saved money by living in the church's small parsonage. That meant on Tuesday morning at 4 A.M. I would leave the house and make a three-hour drive in our Volkswagen Beetle to Denver.

The drive along Route 36 from the Kansas border to Denver was almost a straight shot. As you looked westward to the horizon, you sensed that the car could go in any direction and never run into a barrier. It was smooth sailing.

Life is sometimes like that. No barriers. You feel, *I can do anything I want if I am willing to work hard enough. And pray hard enough. And study hard enough.* I once believed that myself.

But back to Route 36. Just beyond the town of Last Chance, Colorado, you suddenly see three mountain peaks on the horizon — Pike's Peak to the south, Long's Peak to the north, and Mount Evans directly to the west. Instantly the illusion of a barrierless journey is pricked by the realization that three solid and rather large obstacles represent a reduction in options.

Sometimes in ministry we also reach a "Last Chance." The day comes when we discover personal barriers and limits: *I cannot do this as well as . . . I don't actually have the gift of . . . This task requires something that simply isn't my strength.*

Obligations are accrued, perhaps a spouse, maybe a child or two, perhaps responsibilities to extended family members. They wouldn't be complimented by being called barriers. But they nevertheless cut down on other options.

This can be a tough moment for some young leaders. The once dizzying dreams are slowly modified by reality. And little by little we begin to discover why we're really in this "business" of serving God. We're probably not going to be heroes, and the world is not going to beat a path to our door, begging for our insights. And that's okay.

But let me finish my parable.

On the trip to Denver, as you near the city, there comes a point where the long stretch of the Rocky Mountains rises up like an impenetrable wall. Where once only three barriers, evenly spaced apart, interrupted the horizon, now barriers fill your vision. You get the feeling you can't go anywhere. You're *trapped!* The illusion of barrierlessness is inverted.

That's the perception of more than one midlifer in ministry. The freshness is gone; the fears of mediocrity, of ineffectiveness, of being lost in the shuffle are malignant.

Penetrate the curtain of quiet thought of many 40- and 50-year-old pastors, and you will find this wall is a very real perception: *Where can I go? And to whom can I tell this fear that I can't go anywhere? And why do I feel ashamed that I even worry about these things? Would my heroes, then and now, worry about walls? What's wrong with me?*

When you get to your own "Rocky Mountains," you have three choices: (1) try going back to your point of origin, "youthfulness," where the dream of no limits still exists, (2) try driving in circles, cursing the wall and moaning that it's impossible to go back, or, and this is the important possibility, (3) try going up to the wall and find the passes or tunnels that lead to a healthy, spiritually vigorous, and personally effective last forty years of life.

I'm at the point in life where I'm traveling through the wall and enjoying the process! Now I know that life in the "barrierless" days was nice but terribly unrealistic.

No wonder that in those days, the older men never sought me out for wisdom and counsel. They were kind to me, listened to my sermons, followed me when I had good ideas and enthusiasm. But now I know what they were thinking: *He's a good kid who needs to grow a little before he's ready to know our hearts.*

I took my turn driving in circles for a while. In a moment of great personal failure and sadness, I had to drive in circles while

Gail and I sought the voice of the Lord about our future — whether one actually existed or not. These were some of the darkest days of our lives. But they were also days of unforgettable tenderness as God taught us some things through pain that we might not have otherwise learned.

Because God is a kind and gracious God, and because I was surrounded by some men and women who believed in restorative grace, I discovered the future up in the passes and tunnels that lead through the wall.

Elsewhere I've written about the day I was hit with the question: *What kind of an old man do you want to be?* And I opted for growth and grace as my old-age lifestyle. I love the words of Tennyson in his poem "Ulysses." He imagines the old, travel-worn Ulysses brooding on what one might do for an encore after having seen the world:

Tho' much is taken, much abides: and tho'
We are not now that strength which in old days
Moved earth and heaven; that which we are, we are;
One equal temper of heroic hearts,
Made weak by time and fate, but strong in will
To strive, to seek, to find, and not to yield.

That spells it out for me — "strong in will to strive, to seek, to find, and not to yield." Here's an old man who has chosen growth for an old-age lifestyle when other old men were opting to go to Greece's version of Florida and the shuffleboard courts.

Or perhaps I could have used Paul's words — "though our outer man wastes away, our inner man is renewed every day." Again, "I have fought the good fight, I have finished the race." I love the enthusiasm of Tennyson's Ulysses and the feisty Paul.

So at midlife I asked God for a rebirth of spirit and mind. And I found a wonderful liberation: liberation from expectations of the system in which I'd grown up, liberation from feeling I always had to be right and to please everyone's definition of orthodoxy, liberation from always having to be more successful this year than last year, liberation from fearing that some people wouldn't like me — a slow and certain liberation that said, *Be content to be a pleasure to*

Christ, a lover to your wife, a grandfather to your children's children, a friend to those who want to share life with you, and a servant to your generation.

In part that liberation came from the grace and kindness of Jesus and, second, from having to clean up after failure. Those who knew me knew now my worst moments, my most embarrassing failures. I was free now to open my life and be what I was: a sinner who survives only because of the charity of Christ.

Now there is freedom to talk about fears, doubts, disappointments, and weaknesses. Because anything good that comes from someone like me actually comes from God. Paul said it best: "When I am weak, then I am strong."

So when one decides to go through the wall, where do you begin?

A Place to Start

In *Christ-Followers in the Real World,* I wrote about a Sunday morning several years ago when I was in my circle-driving period of life. There was no going back to earlier years, and there was no clear direction for the future.

That Sunday morning I turned on the television and found myself looking at Robert Schuller. The first thing I heard him say was, "I want to talk about enthusiasm." I remember thinking sourly, *The man rarely talks about anything else!*

Then Schuller said, "Most of us think that enthusiasm is the result of circumstances around us. But enthusiasm is that which you choose to generate from within yourself regardless of circumstances."

That was an epiphany moment for me. Instantly I was aware that, for the previous three or four years, I'd been living bereft of any enthusiasm. I had been going through the motions as best as I could. I may sound as if I'm exaggerating, but I felt like a boxer who'd been knocked out but didn't have the sense to fall to the canvas and rest for a while. I presented myself to people as if I were enthusiastic, but a search of the soul revealed that the genuine article just wasn't there.

In that moment I also realized that in our home Gail had been the source of any enthusiasm in our lives for quite some time. And, like a parasite, I'd been drawing energy from her.

I thought about this for a while and then went to Gail.

"I have an apology to make," I told her.

"About what?"

"I've decided to become enthusiastic again."

"Huh?"

"I'm serious. I've been living off your enthusiasm for the last few years, and I have made a decision to become an enthusiastic man again. As of now I'm taking back my share of the responsibility to be enthusiastic in our marriage."

Gail didn't have the slightest idea of what I was talking about, although she had been aware that some life had gone out of me. But she took my word on it. And I went to work to overcome the naturally melancholic, brooding, introverted person that I am. So in my journal I recorded a commitment: to generate enthusiasm from within and spread it.

A Sense of Direction

But being enthusiastic is only a start. The world is full of enthusiastic people. The San Diego Chicken is enthusiastic. So are the guys on television who sell electric juice makers, auto polish, and investment schemes. The question is, *What are you going to be enthusiastic about?*

As a Christ-follower, the answer is about following Christ, growing in godliness, being a servant in his kingdom. But it had to be more specific. What was there that would capture my imagination and generate passion?

I began to wrestle again with the question mentioned earlier: *What sort of an old man do you want to be?* I took a look around and discovered I didn't know many old men who impressed me with the same traits mentioned by Tennyson's Ulysses.

Why? Maybe because most men and women never build a growth plan for the old years. And if you don't plan for the kind of man (or woman) you want to be when you are 80 (God willing) and begin building that when you are 40 or 50, it's not likely to happen.

That's what drove me to define my personal mission. Without a mission, people live by reaction rather than initiation. I'd written a few mission statements for organizations — why not one for myself?

Today my mission statement sits on page two of my journal, where I read it each morning as I start my day. It defines my direction and channels my enthusiasm.

My life is focused on serving God's purposes in my generation so that the Kingdom of Christ might be more firmly established wherever I go. In my dealings with people, I want to be a source of hope, encouragement, enthusiasm, friendship, and service. As a man I seek the daily enlargement of my spirit so that it might be a dwelling place for Christ, a source of wisdom and holiness unto the Lord.

It is a functional statement, describing in broad, macroterms what I want to do with my life. It calls for me to grow by being on a constant search for the purposes of God for the times in which I live. And it puts me squarely on a mission of kingdom building: calling people to the kingdom of God, doing my best to press kingdom conditions into the world in which I live.

It is a statement of quality, reminding me every day of what kind of man I want to be, what I believe Jesus has called me to be: a servant. I know the words are lofty. They're meant to be. A mission that isn't lofty isn't worth pursuing. I want my mind and spirit to be rechallenged every day with what Paul called "the high calling of Christ."

It is also a relational statement. It calls me to high standards as I interact with people, and it describes some of those standards. It outlines what I want to offer in my relationships. More than once I've awakened in a less-than-best mood and grumped a bit at Gail. And then, having successfully grumped, I have turned to my mission statement about hope, encouragement, enthusiasm, friendship, and service. Repentance usually follows.

I've heard people groan about mission statements. "Too managerial," some say. "Not my temperament," says another. "Too broad, too general, too ethereal." But I'm fascinated by a little-known instruction in Deuteronomy 17 where Moses spoke of future kings. Kings, he said, should be careful to do certain things and not do other things (such as have many wives, acquire horses, accumulate gold and silver, or send people back to Egypt).

Then, having issued that warning, Moses said this: "When he takes the throne of his kingdom, he is to write for himself on a scroll a copy of this law, taken from that of the priests. . . . It is to be with him, and he is to read it all the days of his life so that he may learn to revere the Lord his God and follow carefully all the words of this law and these decrees."

Isn't that describing a mission statement? Interesting that he would say the king should "write this for himself." He is to read what he's written every day. Why? Because a king's life is open to all sorts of internal and external seductions and deceits. He needs reminders of where he's supposed to be going and what he is to avoid. Both kings and Christian leaders should construct for themselves such a statement, a covenant of growth.

A Mission Is Not Enough

But a mission statement may not be enough. Early in this quest, I began to think about "sub-missions," equally-lofty goals for each major area of my life. I identified seven areas I really needed to bring under discipline.

Physical: To keep my body healthy, through good habits, regular exercise, prudent nutrition, and weight discipline.

Relational: To love my wife in the pattern of Christ's love, to enjoy her friendship, and to make sure that her quality of life is the best I can make it. It is to be as faithful a family man as possible to my children and my grandchildren. And, finally, to be a vigorous friend to a small circle of men and women to whom I'm drawn in community. Beyond that I want to be a contributing member to my generation, always giving more to people than I take.

Intellectual: To steepen my learning curve whenever possible through reading and exposure to thinking people and disciplines of the day.

Financial: To be generous, debt-free, moderate in expenditure, and careful to plan for the years of my life when income production may be difficult.

Vocational: To represent the purposes of God for my generation and to teach/write as well as model all aspects of "quality of spirit." I would like to make this happen both inside and outside the Christian community.

Spiritual: To be a focused, holy, obedient, and reverent man before God and his world; to discipline my life so that it is controlled by the Spirit within me and so people are drawn one step closer to Christ because of me.

Recreational: To seek restoration in this world by enjoying creation, caring for it, and seeking its reconciliation to the Creator.

I read these statements almost every morning as part of my personal meditations. Several comments about them:

First, they reflect what I personally think God wants from me. I don't compare myself with the apostles and the heroes any more. Their achievements were and are unique, but so are mine. My submissions excite me. I seek a certain nobility in them. They motivate me to a higher way of living.

Second, they represent a variety of dreams, reflecting my life as a whole person: in touch with my body, my friends, my mind, my skills, and my world.

Third, they're flexible. Over the years, I've fine-tuned these statements as I've discovered new interests and abilities.

Finally, they're not crippling dreams. They are open-ended. And they do not produce guilt when I slip backward a bit. But you can be sure that I'm sometimes chided and rebuked when I read them.

Operating Values

The front pages of my journal include one more addition to the mission and sub-mission statements. And these I've come to call my "operating values."

I think Paul was giving Timothy some operating values when he scattered through the epistles those little zingers that give insight into Paul's concerns for his protege: "Let no one despise your youth." You can tell where Paul felt Timothy was weak and vulnerable, where Timothy had some growing to do.

Frankly, there are some habits and weaknesses in my life that are constantly erosive to my pursuit of character. And now that I know that I'm not simply going to outgrow these characteristics, I have to keep preaching to myself with my own set of zingers.

My list of values would not be helpful to anyone else except as samples of what you might want to write for yourself. I don't normally show them, but a few look like this:

● Assume that you are ultimately powerless to manage your life and that you must surrender to heavenly power.

● Live as transparently as possible, resisting image-building.

● Derive self-value from the Creator and not from people or achievements.

● Renounce the instinct to slander or devalue others.

● Insure that your words are positive, seminal, motivational, and lovingly candid.

● Deal ruthlessly with self-deceit and unearned applause.

● Content yourself with "littleness, biddenness, and powerlessness."

● Resist a competitive spirit; permit no inner resentments; rejoice in the success of others.

● Persevere with quality: don't give up or quit easily.

● Keep your "inner springs" clean so that you can "water the earth."

Frankly, a lot of this is difficult to measure. It makes it difficult for us ever to feel as if we've achieved a satisfactory level. (When we're told, "If you think you've arrived, you haven't," I don't know what to do. But I do know that focusing on our values will help us grow.)

Journaling

Over the years I've introduced several other activities to my spiritual disciplines. The first and foremost is journaling.

My journal carries a starting date somewhere in 1968. And since then I've managed to keep a record of almost every day of my life.

I began journaling because I discovered that many of the saints found it profitable. I guess that's one of the times I copied the heroes. The saints and mystics lived without TV, phones, and all the other scintillating interruptions we've allowed into our lives. I found that a commitment to keeping a journal forced me away from the distractions. And it pressed me to think, to evaluate, to reflect, and to remember. It provided a way to look at events and impressions and interpret the presence of God in it all.

Today I write my journal on a laptop computer, a concession to technology. It enables me to write more, do it faster, and to overcome my repugnance toward my own handwriting.

The journal becomes a tool for measuring short-term and long-term growth. The short-term measurements are daily. I frequently end a daily entry into the journal with: "Results today will be measured by . . ." and then I list the things I believe I should accomplish and what it would take to consider those accomplishments as finished. There is a sense of well-being when I go back to that list the next day and type in DONE after each one.

Sometimes I write something as simple as "Enjoy a great afternoon with Gail," or "Review travel schedule and make sure your calender is up to date."

For long-term growth, I use the journal to inquire about the state of my soul (to use older language). What has Scripture been saying to me? What is God saying through my meditations? What feelings, themes, attitudes are predominant these days? Am I fearful, preoccupied, moody, angry? What sensitivities are being stimulated? What new thoughts and concerns might be God's way of directing my life? This stuff has got to be written down in my world, or it just sails right through the conscious mind and leaves, having no effect.

Then I use the journal approximately every four months to evaluate growth and progress. New Year's Day, my birthday (in

April), and the end of vacation (August 30) are usually times to look over the past months and ask the great "Sabbath questions": Where have I been? And has the journey been fruitful? Where should I be going? And do I have the resources to get there?

Are We Ever Fail-Safe?

After all these words about ways of pursuing growth, I must admit there is no guarantee against failure. Some of the best people in biblical history failed — terribly. We love to herald the exploits of those heroes; we need to give equal attention to their ordinariness as sinners. What set them apart, more often than not, was not their great achievements but their repentant and broken spirits. And wasn't it a broken spirit that God said he loved best?

I need to go one step further and note some things about personal growth that seem at first bleak. I've learned the hard way that having a mission statement, a series of sub-missions, goals and values, a process of journaling and evaluation is not a promise of success. I know failure, and I can tell you that there is no human way to insure against it.

The older I become the more I realize my condition as a barbarian loved by my Father. And this may be the most important insight that comes with aging. Almost all old people who are growing have certain common traits. One of them is that they know without equivocation that they are sinners. And they've come to appreciate the central importance of grace.

I once had a friendship with a man in his seventies and eighties. Lee was a godly man who brought the most unusual people to Jesus.

One day we were having breakfast, and Lee told me about a recent trip he'd taken to Boston. "As I drove toward the city," Lee said, "I realized that I was going to be parking my car and walking through the combat zone (Boston's notorious red-light district). So I pulled into a rest stop and had a time of prayer so I could ask God to protect me from temptation when I walked past all those pornography stores and massage parlors."

"Wait a minute, Lee," I interrupted. "I don't want to offend you, but you're 78 years old. Are you telling me that you're concerned about sexual temptation at your age and after all these years of following the Lord?"

Lee looked at me with an intense look in his eyes. "Son, just because I'm old doesn't mean the blood doesn't flow through my veins. The difference between we old men and you young men is this: we know we're sinners. We've had plenty of experience. You kids haven't figured that out yet."

Now, years later, I understand a bit of what the old man was saying. And I understand why old men and women who are growing are among the most gracious and forgiving people there are.

Growth cannot happen without a powerful respect for the reality of indwelling evil and its insidious work through self-deceit. It leads us to lie to God, ourselves, and one another. The spiritual disciplines are designed not only to lead us into the presence of the Father but to sensitize us to the lies we can find so easy to believe.

The leader is constantly the target of the temptations of deceit. We are never far from the statement King Nebuchadnezzar made on the walls of Babylon: "Is not this great Babylon I have built as the royal residence, by my mighty power and for the glory of my majesty?" Look around at some who have been deceived by the success of media ministry, success in fund raising, the sensation found in fast-growing institutions, the money capable of being accumulated through large fees and "love offerings."

Questions That Fight Deceit

Growth cannot happen when the success is superficial and the heart is deceived. In the Bible, deceit was almost always challenged by the power of hard questions. To Cain: "Why is your face downcast?" To Hezekiah: "What did you show the Babylonians in your house?" To Judas: "Why are you here?" To Ananias and Sapphira: "Why have you lied to the Holy Spirit?"

Gail and I have compiled some tough questions to ask ourselves when we think about growth, questions such as:

1. Am I too defensive when asked questions about the use of my time and the consistency of my spiritual disciplines?

2. Have I locked myself into a schedule that provides for no rest or fun times with friends and family?

3. What does my Daytimer say about time for study, general reading, and bodily exercise?

4. What of the quality of my speech? Am I doing a lot of whining and complaining? Am I frequently critical of people, of institutions, of those who clearly do not like me?

5. Am I drawn to TV shows and entertainment that do not reflect my desired spiritual culture?

6. Am I tempted to stretch the truth, enlarge numbers that are favorable to me, or tell stories that make me look good?

7. Am I blaming others for things that are my own fault, the result of my own choices?

8. Is my spirit in a state of quiet so I can hear God speak?

In *Rebuilding Your Broken World*, I recounted the story of Matthias Rust, the young German who piloted a rental plane into the heart of the former Soviet Union and landed in Moscow's Red Square. I've always thought that to be an apt illustration of what can happen to any Christian leader at any time.

The Soviets were sure they had the best systems of air defense in the world. And a teenager penetrated their airspace and taxied up to the front door of the Kremlin. No Christ-following man or woman can feel the confidence that they are growing if they are not living in a perpetual repentance, a holy sorrow that acknowledges that apart from the power and grace of Christ we will succumb to the evil that abides within until the day Christ returns.

Mastering personal growth depends little on our measuring of ourselves against the saints and heroes. There is value in learning from their lives and witness. But they are among the cloud of witnesses about whom the writer in Hebrews spoke. They remain in the stands as we run our leg of the race. We cannot match ourselves against their performances. Rather, our eyes are to be upon the one who runs with us. Thanks be to God that he is alongside when we run, that he hoists us back up when we fall, that he redefines direction when we are lost, that he cheers us on when we grow fatigued, and that he presents us to the Father when we finish the race.

Ministry has an irritating habit of messing up the best laid personal mission statements.

— Mark Galli

Epilogue

As I said in my introduction, my wife just gave me another plant for my office, a peppermint rose-scented geranium. I was determined not to care for it in my usual mercurial ways. So, first thing every morning, I turned on my office lights, switched on the computer, and then watered my plant.

The other day she dropped by the office and looked at my geranium. "You water this every day?" she asked.

"Yes," I said proudly.

"Try every other day, or only when the top soil is dry. Otherwise you'll drown the poor thing."

Personal growth is like that. It's hard to get it just right, and it requires constant adjustments. In print, our authors sound measured and disciplined, as if personal growth is something one decides to do and just does it. They are the first to acknowledge it's not that easy.

Ministry has an irritating habit of messing up the best laid personal mission statements. And even when we find ourselves adhering to our golden plan perfectly, we discover that we're doing a little too much or a touch too little.

Each of these authors has come to recognize, though, that the goal of personal growth is not some perfectly balanced lifestyle in the here and now, but preparing for a perfect relationship in the there and then.

In the meantime we make adjustments, lots of adjustments, in the certainty that God is working in us to will and to act according to his good purpose.